Open Education

How to Reimagine Learning, Ignite Curiosity,
and Prepare Your Kids for Success

MATT BOWMAN
and ISAAC MOREHOUSE

Foreword by Amy Bowman

Open Education
How to Reimagine Learning, Ignite Curiosity, and Prepare Kids for Success

Published by:

ELITE ONLINE PUBLISHING
63 East 11400 South
Suite #230
Sandy, UT 84070
EliteOnlinePublishing.com

ISBN: 978-1-961801-77-6 (ePub)
ISBN: 978-1-961801-78-3 (Paperback)
ISBN: 978-1-961801-79-0 (Audiobook)

EDU017000
EDU051000
EDU021000

Library of Congress Control Number: forthcoming

Printed in the United States of America
Open Education, 224 S Main, #438, Springville, UT 84663
Editing and publishing support provided by The Write Image Consulting, LLC and Write Your Life.

"In a world where education often feels inflexible, Bowman and Morehouse point families to the tools to take charge. Their practical and inspiring guide proves that learning can be both meaningful and liberating, no matter where you start. Open more opportunities for your child with *Open Education*!"

– Connor Boyack, author of the *Tuttle Twins* children's book series and *Passion-Driven Education*

"Education belongs in the hands of the pioneers, not the gatekeepers. This book shows the way forward."

– T.K. Coleman, education entrepreneur and co-host of *The Minimalist* podcast

"Isaac Morehouse's start-ups have helped non-conformist kids reach their potential for many years. Standard classrooms are okay for some kids, but what about your kid? In *Open Education*, Morehouse and Bowman share their educational secrets, wisdom, and optimism."

– Professor Bryan Caplan, Department of Economics, George Mason University

"Learning isn't confined to classrooms anymore. This book shows families how to navigate and combine the rich landscape of educational possibilities, creating customized learning pathways that build upon their children's interests and needs and center their collective aspirations as a family."

– Amy Anderson, Co-founder and Executive Director, ReSchool

PRAISE FOR OPEN EDUCATION

"After analyzing countless school models, I've discovered one undeniable truth: every child is unique. The most effective educational strategies acknowledge and adapt to this reality. The authors offer a practical framework to help families turn this principle into actionable success that will benefit the child's strengths and learning style."

– Deborah Hendrix,
Executive Director, Parents Challenge

"In today's world, difference is valuable. Yet, traditional education often teaches children to fit narrow boundaries rather than develop their unique strengths. *Open Education* shows how we can finally break free from this outdated model, offering practical guidance for families ready to embrace learning that works with their child's natural curiosities rather than against them. This book is a powerful reminder that every child is different, and that's exactly as it should be."

– Amir Nathoo, Founder, Outschool.com

"What if our education system worked *with* human nature instead of *against* it? Through years of research and practice, the authors provide a compelling answer."

– Roger LaMarca, Senior VP of Business,
Great Hearts Online

BONUS

Visit <u>opened.co/book</u> to join the movement
and access additional resources.

"A revolutionary vision made remarkably accessible. The authors show us how to transform education while keeping learners at the center."

– Emily Liebtag, Chief Innovation Officer, Education Reimagined

"Matt has created a fantastic guide to help parents navigate the journey of finding the best educational fit for their children, packed with practical tips every step of the way."

– Jon England, Founder, Education Innovators Association

"Schools juggle a host of competing priorities that often leave real learning as an afterthought. Matt Bowman and Isaac Morehouse offer a refreshing and actionable framework for parents to rethink education. Their approach empowers families to embrace learner-driven paths that prepare kids not just for school, but for life."

– Thomas Arnett, Senior Fellow, Education Research, Clayton Christensen Institute

"One-size-fits-all education is breaking, but top-down reforms won't save it. This book reveals how families and educators are building something better: a flexible, personalized approach that puts learning in the hands of students and their families."

– Michael B. Horn, Co-founder, Clayton Christensen Institute, Author of *From Reopen to Reinvent*

To every parent who continuously wonders if their love,
effort, and decisions will lead their children to
enjoy a happy, successful life.
You are not alone.

TABLE OF CONTENTS

Foreword by Amy Bowman i

Introduction v

    Education is Opening Up vi

    A Little Bit About Matt and Isaac ix

    Matt & Amy's Journey: How OpenEd Began xvi

PART I

Chapter 1: The Two-Hundred-Year-Old Trap 1

    The Hidden Cost of "Free" Education 5

    The Launch (and Failure) of "No Child Left Behind" 8

    It's Easy to Predict Test Scores 10

    The Post-COVID Awakening 12

    The Homeschool Pioneers of Open Education 14

Chapter 2: Students Are Not Standard 19

    Can Fish Climb Trees? 20

    Meeting Standardized Testing Head On 22

    The Myth of Standardization as Rigor 25

    The Student as a Product 29

    The Education Transparency Problem 30

Chapter 3: "Mastered" or "Not Yet?"......................35

Rethinking What Mastery Means 37

The Three Elements to Real Learning 39

The Freedom to Be Less Than Perfect 42

Reimagine What's Possible. 44

PART II

Chapter 4: Five Building Blocks for an Open Education Mindset...51

The Christiansen Solution 51

Becoming an Open Education Designer. 61

Chapter 5: Building Block #1: Embrace Your Child's Uniqueness...63

What is Average? 63

The Myth of the Average Student 66

Chapter 6: Building Block #2: Put Your Kids Before Your Reputation 73

The Powerful Force of Social Pressure. 73

Chapter 7: Building Block #3: Map the Learning Landscape...79

Three Elements of Learning 79

Connecting Interests, Needs, and Resources to Learning . 80

Step 2: Identify Needs. 85

Step 3. Analyze Available Resources. 89

Chapter 8: Building Block #4: Give Your Child a Voice . . .103

Minecraft as Education? 103

Rekindle Your Child's Curiosity 105

Trust Them to Find Their Own Way. 107

Unwind the Great Rewiring 109

Building Blocks of Agency: Love, Limits, and Latitude . . 114

The Science and Art of Play. 116

When Concepts Meets Reality: Addressing Common
Concerns 118

**Chapter 9: Building Block #5: Celebrate Learner-driven
Sprints** 123

The Secrets of Pacing 123

It's Not About the Speed 124

The Anatomy of a Sprint 126

Learner-Driven Sprints 127

PART III

Chapter 10: Open Education Pathways After High School . . 135

Real Life Teaching 135

Entrepreneurship Inspires Learning. 137

Start with Why. 139

Southern New Hampshire University (SNHU-CBE)
and OpenEd 142

Alternative Paths to Success: What's Old is New Again . . 146

**Chapter 11: Beyond the Box: The Great Education
Unbundling** 155

The Cost of Education 155

Escape the False Binary of Education Choice. 157

Trust in the Learning Marketplace. 165

Chapter 12: Building Your Open Education Plan 169

Lessons Learned from The LEGO Movie 169

Building Your Own Open Education Plan 171

Sample Plans Based on Real Families 175

Making it Click Together 185

Conclusion: You Can Do This (You Already Are) **189**

An Ode to Sir Ken Robinson 189

About the Author: Matt Bowman **195**

About the Author: Isaac Morehouse **197**

Acknowledgments **199**

End Notes **201**

STUDENTS AREN'T STANDARD

One evening, when our youngest daughter was about seven, she skipped into our bedroom just to tell us she was going to read a book. As she skipped back out, I turned to my husband, Matt, and asked, "At what point does life take that skip out of you? When do we lose that pure joy in learning?" That question has stuck with me ever since.

Too often, I have seen how our traditional education system slowly replaces that natural joy with rigid expectations and standardized measures. As we raised our five children—all in the same home environment and with the same routines, house rules, and opportunities—we noticed something that every parent before us already knew: each child is profoundly different. But what struck me wasn't just their different personalities or interests, it was how differently each one learned and developed.

Like many parents, we started with traditional approaches. I volunteered at the local public school and ran the book fair. Matt coached every sport until our kids were teenagers. We did all the "right" things. But our perspective began to shift when our oldest son wanted to transfer to a brand-new charter school, something almost unheard of in our community at the time. Back then, leaving your assigned district school was seen as a rejection of public education. The pushback was immediate. "What are you doing?"

people asked. "Do you even understand what you're giving up?" We were more concerned about our child feeling validated and successful than following the expected path. Each year we asked if he wanted to return to his district school. He chose to stay, and he thrived. Later, when our younger children reached the same age, they chose a different path entirely. Each choice was different, but each was right for that child.

During this time, we sat down with a calculator and made a startling discovery. Our children spent about seven hours a day in school for 180 days, roughly 1,260 hours per year. That left 2,390 hours of potential learning time at home. The math was undeniable. Time spent outside the classroom matters. Parents are ultimately their children's primary educators, whether they plan for it or not. This realization led us to ask a bigger question. If our own children need more flexible, personalized education options, how many other families face the same challenge?

In 2009, we created My Tech High (now OpenEd) to help students access different classes, resources, and opportunities that spoke to their individual interests and learning styles. Years later, our conviction about personalized learning was reinforced in a deeply personal way. One of our sons was everything the public school system could want. He was a student body officer, a top varsity athlete in multiple sports, and he earned excellent grades. He was well-rounded, well-liked, and loved to learn. Yet, when it came time to take the ACT, he consistently scored below what colleges expected, despite multiple attempts. Watching him pour his heart and soul into studying, only to feel crushed by the results again and again, confirmed what we already knew. Standardized testing measurements can never capture a child's true potential nor accurately reflect what they have learned.

During this journey, I felt God speaking to me, helping me understand something crucial: God is the author of diversity. A child's learning style isn't a flaw to be corrected by the system, it's a divine design to be celebrated. Each child's unique way of learning is beautiful, intentional, and worthy of honor. This understanding transformed how we saw education itself.

One year, we were excited to see several OpenEd students earn their associate degree before they turned eighteen. Matt suggested we might want to host an event to celebrate this major accomplishment. I asked him, "Who decides which achievements are worthy of celebration? Why not host an event to celebrate students who started their own business, or mastered a musical instrument, or achieved their academic goals in their own personal way through art, dance, sports, or an industry certification?" We've been guided by this perspective ever since.

Today, at various in-person OpenEd events, parents I have never met approach me with tears in their eyes, grateful that their children finally have the freedom to learn in ways that work for them. I'll never forget one parent who shared with me that her eight-year-old son was deeply discouraged. He was profoundly gifted in science and was convinced he had learned everything there was to know. He believed his local school had no more challenges to offer him. When he was given the opportunity to attend a college physics class with his grandfather, the professor opened his eyes to ongoing discoveries in quantum mechanics and dark matter. His natural curiosity reignited, and he realized that human knowledge wasn't finite. We're all still learning, still discovering. This changed his life forever.

As a teenager, my father encouraged me to become an expert in something people would seek out. I struggled with that advice as I thought every field of expertise was already claimed. Now I see the irony. Through building OpenEd, I have been fortunate to become an expert in finding ways to help families trust their instincts about their children's education. Today, even as two of our own children are public school teachers, we understand that education isn't about choosing between traditional and alternative approaches, it's about having the confidence to combine different learning opportunities in ways that work for your unique child. That's Open Education.

This book offers a roadmap for that journey. Matt and Isaac break down the practical insights and systematic approach we've developed over fifteen years of working with families who want more for their children. The tools to build something better are already in your hands, and they're simpler to adopt than you might think.

– Amy Bowman, Co-founder, OpenEd,
mother of five children (all married),
Grammy to four grandchildren

INTRODUCTION

"What about socialization?"
"Won't my child fall behind academically?"
"What about college?"
"They'll just play games all day!"
"They need to learn discipline."
"My spouse and I already struggle with our children over homework. Won't this be worse?"
"They won't learn the basics."

If you've ever considered trying something different when it comes to education, you've likely thought or heard these objections. They may have stopped you from making a change. These worries might have led you to feel resigned to a less-than-stellar school experience for your kids.

They shouldn't.

We'll address each one of these common concerns (and more!) and officially invite you to start today to think differently about your child's education.

Education can be so much better than what most of us accept. We want to show you just how easy and accessible a world-class education is when you open up your thinking.

Education is Opening Up

Did you know that the average American child will spend around 15,000 hours in a traditional school classroom by the time they graduate from high school? That's 15,000 hours in a system where two-thirds of teachers are dissatisfied, parent satisfaction is at a twenty-five-year low, and student anxiety, bullying, and depression are rising at an alarming rate. In other words, traditional schooling isn't working well for most kids and almost nobody is happy. For some reason, we have accepted this as normal. But normal doesn't mean necessary.

Many kids start out loving school with the excitement of learning, making friends, discovering new ideas. But something changes, often around 3rd grade. There's a reason for this shift, which will become clear in the chapters ahead.

Fortunately, education is opening up.

For the first time in history, every approach to learning is becoming available to every family. From traditional classrooms to innovative programs and from hands-on apprenticeships to creative career exploration, these options aren't just limited to the wealthy or well-connected. They are now available to everyone.

This means you can shape your child's education around their natural curiosity, interests, and learning style. You can adapt and adjust their learning environment as they grow and change. Most importantly, you can help them maintain that early love of learning that too often gets lost in traditional schools.

⟶ ———————— ⟵

"Where do you go to school?"

This is a seemingly-simple question that many adults might ask a young person in the grocery store, at the park, or at family gatherings. However, it's a hard question for families who have adopted an open education mindset to answer succinctly. Here's how one 16-year-old girl responded to a family friend from another state:

"Well, I'm not sure how to exactly answer your question. I'm taking a science class at my local district school and I'm on the volleyball team there. I also take a few online early college courses from a virtual charter school (and they pay for my tuition). On Mondays, I go to a nearby homeschool co-op to participate in a book club. I have a tutor for math through Outschool.com on Tuesdays and Thursdays, and I work part-time three mornings a week at a local bakery. On Fridays, I mostly 'unschool,' following my own interests and learning by doing."

So… what would you call this educational experience? She didn't really know what to call it, but she knew she loved it. We call it open education.

This approach is becoming more and more common.

The old lines are blurring. The labels are fraying at the edges.

Public, private, homeschool, unschool, large school, microschool, co-op, independent, accredited, non-accredited, in the classroom, out of the classroom, traditional, charter, modern, classical, Montessori, Waldorf, virtual, real-world, synchronous, asynchronous. Parents used to have to carefully pick and get stuck in one box. Now, every one of those boxes is opening up. You can take individual items out of them and craft an educational experience for each child at each stage based on their unique interests and needs.

What does an open education look like? In a nutshell, it is different for each child.

The need to personalize education is rooted in the way humans learn and have always learned. The last 100 years have been, in some ways, a grand social experiment of a factory-style, one-size-fits-all, lump-of-dough education which has left many students behind.

People have a love/hate relationship with school because learning is lovely but school is often loathsome, certainly when it is forced upon people in a cold, conveyor-belt manner—treating every student as an identical product to be processed in exactly the same way.

This book is about the opening up of education. It is about a growing movement, the principles behind it, and the stories of families who are a part of that movement. Beyond that, it is about a mindset. We call it the open education mindset. It's about seeing the world in a different way. Seeing the world as full of possibility. Seeing your child's education as something that *can* be changed, that *can* be improved, that *can* be customized. It's about seeing every option that is available to you. Once you begin to see education with an open mind, you can't help but open your child's education.

Let's be clear, this is not an anti-public-school book, an anti-private school book, or an anti-anything book. It is a book about helping you craft the best possible education for your child by opening up all the available options.

If you are ready for a practical guide to raising self-directed learners who are creative, curious, and motivated to succeed and live happily—today and in the future—this is the book for you. This isn't some new-fangled, made-up, fringe way to teach your kids stuff they don't need to know, might never use, or will hate learning. Instead, open education is a proven approach to give you and your children the power to direct, adjust, and navigate their learning in a way that works best for them.

Although this might seem like a no-brainer (of course you want this for your child), like many parents, you know it isn't easy to accomplish. Every parent wants to see their children enjoying learning, seeking opportunities to grow their knowledge of the world, enhancing their natural intellectual abilities, and sharing what they learn with others. If your family isn't there yet, keep reading. As you do, you may begin to question many deeply-held societal expectations, pressures, and traditions around learning. You

> *Open education is a proven method to give you and your children the power to direct, adjust, and navigate their learning in a way that works best for them.*

might even feel some anger that causes you to ask yourself, "Why didn't anyone tell me this before?"

We will help you through this emotional roller coaster. By the end of the book, you will have the tools and confidence to apply this modern approach to education and tap into all the learning resources available to help your child succeed.

There are innumerable resources at your disposal to enhance your child's learning; you just need to know what they are. As you identify these learning resources and opportunities, you will start to realize the power of an open education mindset, and you may never view schooling the same again. As you make this shift, you may feel scared that you might fail at this new approach to your child's learning path. After all, you will be going against the grain of traditional schooling and that will undoubtedly cause some push-back from your inner circle. As a result, you might think that no matter what you do for your child, someone will judge you, including yourself, other parents, grandparents, and neighbors. That's okay. Keep doing what's right for you and your family.

There is no denying the results of a child learning with an open education mindset. Here, you will read the stories of many real-life families who apply the open education mindset with great results. Every family situation is different, so each idea can be adapted to individual circumstances, all with outcomes that illustrate the benefits of this revolutionary approach to learning. You will also be introduced to two fictional families who might seem familiar to you in some ways. Neither family is perfect or ideal, but their family circumstances, challenges, questions, concerns, and decisions are universal in many ways. In fact, both authors have experienced them personally.

A Little Bit About Matt and Isaac

We (Matt Bowman and Isaac Morehouse) have different backgrounds and different points of emphasis when it comes to education, yet both of us share the open education mindset.

Matt was educated in the public school system and later worked in it for years. He has an abiding love for public education and is passionate about seeing it become the best version of itself. He's spent years advocating for competency-based education, a move away from standardized testing, and ways for public schools to innovate and create public/private partnerships to serve *all* students better.

Isaac grew up homeschooled and has focused his career on ways to innovate outside of the system and build alternatives. He's spent years advocating for apprenticeships, hands-on learning, and ways for individuals to chart a course without relying on mainstream institutions.

Both of us are moved by the same vision. We want to open education for every learner. That includes every type of approach and option available.

Matt's Story

As my wife, Amy, mentioned in the foreword, all five of our children are very different from each other even though they were raised in a fairly consistent household. This taught us that if two parents raising five children in the same way could identify very different pathways for each child, how could a standardized public education system even begin to meet the varied needs of millions of children? Spoiler alert: it can't, at least not by itself. The public education system needs to find ways to partner with innovative, forward-thinking organizations and to work with parents to personalize education for *every* child.

In the early days, our approach was typical of many families around us. We visited the public library frequently for free story time, free book check-out, free audiobooks, and more. We enrolled our children in the free public school near our home. Amy, who chose to be a stay-at-home mom, volunteered at the school, and helped run the book fair. She purchased affordable summer reading and math books at Costco. She also supported the children when they participated in recreation programs like swimming, soccer, and flag football. I volunteered as a coach which included a discounted fee for the kids' registration and uniforms. Like most parents, we were trying our best, but missed the mark many times along our children's learning journeys.

Then, as the internet expanded, we found high-quality online educational games and interesting resources to supplement everything the children were learning in their public school classrooms. Even though we created consistent routines and provided similar opportunities to all our children, each one gravitated toward different activities and learning styles. What worked brilliantly for one would fall completely flat for another. We discovered firsthand what would become the foundation of our educational philosophy. There is no such thing as an "average" child.

> *There is no such thing as an "average" child.*

As mentioned earlier, once we realized how much time our children spent at home versus in their traditional public school inspired us to embrace the many learning opportunities our children had available *outside* of school. We quickly recognized that learning happens everywhere, all the time, in ways as unique as each child.

My parents were both educators, so education is deeply rooted in my soul. I have also always enjoyed exploring entrepreneurial opportunities (i.e., see a need, fill a need) and I started my first education company at 17. After graduating with a bachelor's degree in elementary education, I began my professional teaching career as a 6th grade teacher in Washington state. During that time, I earned my master's degree in education with an emphasis in public school choice models. Then, in 1996, the state announced a grant to bring this new thing called the internet into the classroom. As you can imagine, most teachers balked at the idea, but I jumped on it because it sounded exciting. The internet turned out to be a pretty cool thing and I've been involved with innovation in education, online learning, public school choice, technology, and entrepreneurship ever since.

My experience as a public school teacher helped us understand how to think differently about what, when, and how our children learned. Amy's college degree in accounting helped us manage our family finances as we made important decisions and trade-offs over the years. But even without a background or degree in education and accounting, every parent quickly realizes that children are born with all kinds of interests and skills. An important role of the parent is to provide love, guidance, and support to each child as they learn to thrive in their unique way.

This background in education innovation, combined with our experience raising five unique children, helped us understand something crucial. While professional expertise can be valuable, the most important qualification of an adult to guide a child's education is simply caring deeply about that individual child.

Isaac's Story

My dad was an accountant and my mom was a young public school teacher. When kids came, they decided she would become a full-time mom and they would homeschool. This was in the 1980s, when homeschooling was pretty rare and legally dubious.

I was the youngest of three, and when I was just three years old, my dad was in a serious car accident that left him brain damaged and permanently wheelchair-bound. He required (and does to this day) 24-hour care. My mom decided to continue homeschooling us, even while taking care of a handicapped husband and running the household alone.

This upbringing taught me a great deal of independence and responsibility from a young age. I always had household chores and started earning money from various jobs early. Ever the optimist, my mom instituted a rigorous curriculum and bought more books at curriculum fairs than I could count. In practice, besides homeschool classes and co-ops, our education was pretty *laissez faire.* I played with LEGO bricks more than I did workbooks. Even still, we had a very robust social life, played sports, and did a lot with our church, extended family, and a network of local homeschoolers.

In my early teens, I wanted to hang out with my friends more and join a competitive basketball team. I decided to enroll in a small private school for my sophomore year. While I enjoyed the sports and social aspect, I chafed against the rigid schedule and uniform pace of learning. Why should every student's day be dictated by the same bell when we had radically different abilities and interests? The pace felt slow and unnatural. I also disliked having only a few hours left to work and earn money.

During my junior and senior years, I attended community college full-time while working part-time. The curriculum was better than high school and more customizable, but most classes felt like busy work. I finished high school with an associate degree and transferred the credits to the local state university. I earned my bachelor's degree in two years there, wondering the entire time why I was paying all this money for classes nobody seemed to want to attend (including the professors). I worked nearly full-time throughout, learning more on the job than I did in the classroom. This really bugged me, and I resolved to find a better way to help young people transition from education to career, without all the debt and waste.

I got started on my career, bought a house, got married, and had my first child by the time I was 21. A few years later, after taking night classes, I earned a master's degree. If you're wondering about the need for test scores and diplomas, I never got a high school diploma or GED and I never took the ACT or SAT, but I have an associate, bachelor's, and master's degree— none of which really helped me in real life, to be honest—and a great career.

I loved growing up homeschooled and the independence that came with it. It was a no-brainer for my wife, Heather, and me to homeschool our own kids. But we were young and naive and hadn't thought too hard about what that would look like. We began with a very structured and full curriculum for our oldest. He was smart and verbally advanced, so we figured it would be great to start him at 4 ½ years old. It wasn't.

He fought us at every turn. He wanted to play, imagine, draw, and tell stories. He did not want to be told what to do or when to do it. When it came to reading, for example, we tried every method, but he wouldn't accept any of the learning activities we presented to him. We knew he was capable. Finally, we gave up and decided to let him learn whenever he wanted to. Not long after, he taught himself. One night he wanted me to read to him in bed, but I said no. It was late and I was exhausted. I walked past his room a little later and heard him reading to himself. A lightbulb went on in my mind. *Maybe we should just let him choose what and when he wants to learn. If he needs help, he'll ask us.* That experience, coupled with devouring books from thinkers like John Holt, John Taylor Gatto, and Peter Gray, and learning about the Sudbury Valley School, led us to go full unschool.

As we had more kids (one adopted, two more biological) and they grew and developed, our education approach was forced to change too. We saw needs and gaps and desires they had that required more structure. Over the years, we had them in homeschool tutorials and co-ops, various at-home and online curricula, a twice-a-week microschool, a part-time Waldorf school, and every variation in between. One year, our oldest wanted to go to a public high school, so we let him. He decided not to go back the next year and instead to work full time, so we let him do that, too.

These were not easy decisions and we never fully felt we knew what we were doing (we still don't have all the answers) but one major lesson along the way has been humility. We had to swallow a lot of pride to admit our fancy curriculum wasn't working. We'd gone from a fully structured curriculum to a fully unschooled model for all our kids. But this didn't solve every problem for every kid every year. Besides that, we had to face lots of raised eyebrows and social pressure too. Then, after I had become an outspoken advocate for unschooling and alternative approaches to education, I had to swallow my pride again when more structure was needed, and my son enrolled in public school. This time, I faced skeptical questions from my network of alt-educators.

The real lesson is that it's not about us, the parents. It's not about what I think sounds good or makes me look good. It's about what best helps my kids. There is a lot of 'dying to self' in this process, but in the end, the rewards are more than worth it.

> *There is no such thing as an "average" child.*

While my wife primarily managed our kids' education, I started a few companies dedicated to that goal I had way back in college. I wanted to help young people successfully transition from student to professional. I worked with lots of great people, serving hundreds of individuals with bootcamps, apprenticeships, alternative credentials, and software tools to launch their careers. Along the way, I met Matt and learned about his company, OpenEd (which at the time was called My Tech High). We came at it from different angles, but our vision was the same. We hit it off and kept in touch for nearly a decade. When he approached me about joining the OpenEd team it was the perfect next step for me and a chance to be a "pioneer of the inevitable," as my friend TK Coleman says.

Between my wife and me, and our four children, we have participated in just about every form of education there is. Public, private, homeschool, unschool, and everything in between. The labels and theories aren't the most important thing. What matters is the opportunity for each child to craft the education combination that works for them at each stage. We're still on that journey, so I don't write as someone who has figured it all out, only as someone who is learning out loud in hopes that my experiences will help others.

Through our own journey, we've seen how many parents are searching for alternatives. We've noticed a marked increase lately in how many parents at the park might say something like, "I'm just not sure about Johnny. He's not doing great in school, but what can we do?" Parents know something is wrong, but they are worried they will ruin their kids' lives if they pull them out of the system and customize their education. They feel they aren't equipped, and they have tons of "what ifs."

My wife, Heather, comes home more frequently than ever relaying comments like this. What's amazing is how often it only takes a few simple words to take these parents from curiosity to courage and conviction when it comes to opening their kids' education. Heather usually asks a few questions, then says something simple like, "Well, I can tell you our kids are not perfect, and their education isn't perfect, but it's easier than you think to take charge and do something different. It's okay. You're not going to ruin their lives. Why don't you just try opening things up?" Those words have a magical effect. It's like a burden is lifted and they have permission to consider a different approach for the first time. There are millions of parents who want to open their kids' education and just need a little encouragement and to know it's going to be okay. If that's you, we hope this book can help.

Open education is my mission and passion.

Matt & Amy's Journey: How OpenEd Began

One day we (Matt and Amy) were having a conversation with our middle son about the charter school he attended with his two older brothers. He opened up to us and said, "I really don't want to go to this school anymore. I want to transfer back to my district school to be with my friends."

At first, we thought he should just stick it out and stay with his brothers. If we transferred him to his district school, we would literally have our five children attending four different public schools and we thought that would be too logistically challenging. After thinking about it, we concluded we could make it work as we genuinely wanted to honor his preference.

The experience of supporting our children in accessing an education environment that worked for them prepared us for when we launched OpenEd.

As our knowledge about how our kids learn grew, we sought insights from other parents on what they found worked or didn't work well for their child. We (again) learned that every child is unique, each family's situation is different, and it takes a lot of focused energy to prioritize adjusting the family's education plan around the needs of each child. With that knowledge, we worked to identify each child's needs and interests and discover which resources we could source to help them thrive.

At the height of these important and meaningful discussions around designing open education plans for our five children, we felt divine inspiration to share our personal and professional experiences with other families. OpenEd was born, built on the foundation of what we call the open education mindset, a groundbreaking, yet time-honored approach to self-directed learning that allows children to choose their own learning journey with the input, feedback, and support of parents and other caring adults who know the child the best.

When we began this journey in 2009, we called the program My Tech High, as we were focused on helping 16-17-year-old students become tech entrepreneurs and launch their own tech companies. To our core, we believed then (and still believe) that if all children have some level of confidence and competence in both how technology works and how to think like an entrepreneur, they can be successful in life no matter what path they chose to follow. Originally, we thought our students would be able to follow in the footsteps of modern tech titans like Bill Gates, Steve Jobs, Ursula Burns, Mark Zuckerberg, Larry Page, and Sergey Brin. However, as it turned out, the average age of our My Tech High students in the first year was nine years old, and the most eager to learn new things were the 10-14-year-olds (as the older students felt so much societal pressure to focus only on college prep).

This unexpected development led us to a profound realization that although technology and entrepreneurship remained vital tools, our mission was actually much broader. We weren't just teaching tech skills; we were empowering families to direct their own educational journeys. This understanding led us to rename our program OpenEd, reflecting our expanding vision of education as an experience that should be open, flexible, and accessible to all learners in whatever way works best for them.

We shifted our focus to help younger students thrive in an open education format and saw amazing results. We discovered five-year-olds learning to code, six-year-olds starting their own t-shirt businesses, and more. Over time, we expanded to include early college and career pathways for older students.

Our mission became clear. We wanted to expand access to high-quality, personalized education to all families, regardless of income. Rather than create something entirely outside the traditional system (as many education reformers advised), we partnered with forward-thinking public schools to offer flexible education options. Working with innovative charter schools and district leaders, we have demonstrated what is possible when we transform education from within the existing system.

Through our programs and partnerships, OpenEd cumulative enrollment has exceeded 100,000 students and continues to grow rapidly. With each new family, we have refined our understanding of what open education truly is. It is a proven method that gives parents and children the power to direct, adjust, and navigate learning in ways that work best for them.

> *OpenEd cumulative enrollment has exceeded 100,000 students and continues to grow rapidly.*

The path hasn't been easy. Not everyone in the traditional education system embraces personalized education. We have faced opposition, legal challenges, nasty and personal attacks, and moments of deep doubt. During the COVID-19 pandemic in 2020, when enrollment suddenly skyrocketed, we faced a crucial decision: scale back or step up. We chose to keep our doors open to anyone interested, recognizing that the crisis of that moment called for exactly the kind of flexible, personalized approach we had spent years developing.

We imagine a world where families don't have to pick from one pre-defined education approach, where learners can blend real-world connection with the flexibility of digital learning, where technology and entrepreneurship are embraced and wielded for good, and where every student develops independence and the ability to solve the biggest problems.

This is the essence of open education—recognizing that each student's path is unique, that the world is full of possibilities, and that learning thrives when students can break free from artificial constraints. Rather than being forced to choose between public or private, remote or on-site, part-time or full-time, large or small classes, homeschool or world school, or any other approach, open education allows learners to take what works from any of them and adapt it to their goals. It opens every parent and student to whatever combination of resources and methods they need, when and how they need them.

Is This Book For You?

If you're already exploring open education, don't underestimate the power of your experience. Your story, even with its imperfections and ongoing questions, could be exactly what another parent needs to hear. Part of this book's mission is to help you grow in your journey while equipping you to support others just beginning to question the status quo.

And if you've picked up this book because something isn't working in your child's education—whether it's a dimming love of learning, a rigid system that constrains rather than enables, or a sense that there must be a better way—you're in the right place. This book exists to help resolve that nagging dissatisfaction with the educational status quo.

Read on if:

- Your child is unhappy at school and you want to reignite their love of learning.
- You are unsatisfied with your child's current schooling experience and the dissatisfaction is too painful to continue as is.
- You believe schooling, work, and life are supposed to be joyful and meaningful.
- You are mentally and emotionally strong enough to change and are open to learning other pathways to becoming a successful and happy adult.
- You are comfortable questioning long-established institutions.
- You are ready to get out of the daily rat race and find more peace and joy as a parent.
- You already have an open education mindset and want to learn even more ideas for what you can do.

Yes, going against the grain can feel daunting. Friends, family, even well-meaning teachers might question your choices. But what we've discovered, after working with tens of thousands of families, is that once parents see learning through an open lens, they can never go back to viewing education the same way. What happens when we stop trying to standardize children and start embracing their natural genius? What becomes possible when we break free from a system designed for a world that no longer exists? The answer might surprise you. More importantly, it might forever transform how your child experiences learning.

Let's begin by understanding the trap that has held education captive for nearly two centuries, and why now is the perfect moment to break free.

PART I

CHAPTER 1:

THE TWO-HUNDRED-YEAR-OLD TRAP

Horace Mann stood before the Massachusetts legislature with an ambitious vision. As Secretary of the Massachusetts Board of Education, he had been molding the state's schools for many years into a model of an educational system he had never seen firsthand. It wasn't until 1843 that Mann actually travelled to Europe to observe the infamous "Prussian model of education"—a system explicitly designed to produce obedient soldiers and loyal citizens through rigid standardization and discipline.

Mann returned from his seven-day trip convinced of the Prussian model's merits. He was less impressed with the quality of learning than the efficiency of control. Here was a system that could take diverse, independent-minded children and transform them into a uniform, compliant workforce. American industrialists loved the idea. Factory bosses needed workers who would follow instructions without question, arrive punctually, and adhere to rigid schedules.

And so began what we now know as modern public education, not with dreams of expanding human potential, but with plans to standardize it. Massachusetts passed America's first compulsory school attendance law in 1852, and the model spread rapidly across the northern states.

Perhaps the most telling aspect of the factory model of education was how it came to grade students using the same A to F scale that meat packers used for beef. Just as Grade-A meat commanded premium prices, while lower grades were deemed less desirable, students would be sorted and labeled according to their ability to conform. The system sorted children by manufacture date (what we now call grade levels), processed them into batches, and tested their conformity at regular intervals. Those who didn't fit the mold were labeled as troublemakers or failures. This wasn't some secret conspiracy. It was all quite open, quite logical . . . for a world built around factories and mass production.

The wealthy families, of course, kept their children out of this new public system. Their kids continued learning through mentors, tutors, and rich experiences through an education designed to produce leaders rather than followers. For everyone else, school became what Mann and his industrial partners intended. It was a place where unique human beings would be standardized into interchangeable parts.

> *The wealthy families, of course, kept their children out of this new public system.*

Even today, this system directly shapes the lives of our children. Every weekday morning, millions of unique young minds file into buildings designed to make them more alike. The seemingly simplicity of the promise remains seductive. If we want to be successful, we are told, just follow the predetermined path of getting good grades, going to college, working a steady job and then retiring. It's a promise whispered to parents at every PTA meeting and open house; just trust the system and your child will thrive. That promise has expired not only because it is failing to deliver for many kids, but also because it's preparing our children for a world that has already disappeared.

For over a century, this system worked exactly as intended. But in the last few decades, parents and teachers began noticing that young minds don't flourish on assembly lines. Students are not dead meat. We are still using an education system designed before the lightbulb was invented to prepare children for a future that includes such modern advances as artificial intelligence, robotics, self-driving vehicles, the blockchain, and 3D printing. A system created for factory workers cannot possibly prepare children for jobs that don't even exist yet. It would be comical if it weren't impacting millions of young lives.

What makes this especially painful is watching the tension between how children naturally learn and how they are forced to learn. Any parent who has seen their child master a complex video game, build elaborate worlds in Minecraft, or dive deep into a passion project, knows that kids are capable of extraordinary learning when it matters to them. Yet, the education system insists on grading these dynamic, creative minds like sides of beef in a meat packing plant: Grade A for above average, or Grade F for substandard, with no room for growth or transformation. The cracks in this system are becoming impossible to ignore. Some students, unable to conform to the standardized pace, are labeled as failures despite their unique talents. Others, capable of moving much faster, are held back by arbitrary age groupings. Both ends of this spectrum arrive at the same conclusion: something needs to change.

Parents—especially those who remember their own joy of learning before school squeezed it out of them—have started pushing back against the birth-year cohort model, where children are grouped in a classroom based on their birth year, not by their capabilities or interests. This revolution has unfolded in almost every other aspect of our lives. Think about how you consume entertainment now compared to 40 years ago when there were only three TV channels. Or how you now might work remotely instead of commuting to a cubicle, which was commonplace less than a decade ago. Yet somehow, society has kept our children trapped in an educational model more rigid than the factories it was designed to supply.

The 1990s marked a turning point. Parents and educators from across the political spectrum, united by their concern for children rather than ideology, began demanding choice within the public system itself. They weren't asking to abandon public education. They were asking to open it up, to make it flexible enough to serve real children rather than theoretical averages. This wasn't just about choosing between public and private schools, a choice that, let's be honest, has always existed for families with means. This was about reimagining what public education could be. Magnet schools, charter schools, hybrid programs, and customized learning plans started emerging like flowers breaking through cracks in concrete.

What drove this movement was a growing recognition that children are as unique in how they learn as they are in how they look, laugh, or dream. Some need more time with certain subjects while they race ahead in others. Some learn best through books, others through hands-on experience. Some thrive in traditional classrooms, while others come alive in alternative settings. The standardized system didn't just fail to recognize these differences, it actively worked to eliminate them.

Informed by Mann's goal to mirror the meat-grading model onto children, and under the guise of tax dollar accountability, test scores inappropriately became the chosen metric for K-12 public education accountability. Using arbitrary scores through standardized testing as a way to measure children's educational development was, and still is, misguided, misdirected, and frankly inequitable. No other government program even comes close to requiring similar metrics to justify its existence or its massive spending.

For example, trillions of public dollars are spent each year on Medicare,

> *Using arbitrary scores through standardized testing as a way to measure children's educational development was, and still is, misguided, misdirected, and frankly inequitable.*

Medicaid, Pell Grants, scholarships, and college financial aid to name a few. However, none of these programs impose standardized accountability tests upon the beneficiary to justify their spending. Our point here is not to support or oppose these programs, nor to hold them up as examples of efficiency or outcomes, but to highlight how public education is treated in a wildly different manner than other public services.

Imagine if any citizen who received government funding for healthcare was measured to see how tall they were, and any healthcare facility that didn't have a majority of patients at the predetermined height was threatened with loss of funds. While height might be a useful health metric for some people in some cases, the idea of applying it across the board is absurd. Yet this is exactly the kind of accountability that is used with public spending on education. The problem is not with the concept of accountability, but where the accountability comes from, who is accountable to whom, and what kind of incentives exist within the system to allow for adjustment and adaptation. Our contention is that whoever is closest to the student is best positioned to determine what "good" looks like; the students themselves and their parents being first and foremost. Family, friends, teachers, and community members close to them come next. County, state, and finally federal level bureaucrats are increasingly far removed from this context, and therefore are worst positioned to determine accountability metrics.

The Hidden Cost of "Free" Education

Derrell Bradford, president of 50CAN: The 50-State Campaign for Achievement, is a rare advocate for both school choice and improving the public schools. He reminds people that public schools are not, in fact, tuition free. In practice, home prices act as tuition. To access higher quality schools, you have to pay more for houses in those districts. This is one of the reasons he supports opening up more choices in education.

The people who continue to oppose offering public school choices to all students are often those who can comfortably afford to buy a home in a district with top-notch, well-funded public schools. These elite, "public schools" in wealthy neighborhoods actually act more like quasi-private schools, fully subsidized by the government through the high property taxes generated by expensive homes. Restrictive closed enrollment policies also allow these so-called public schools to deny enrollment to students whose families cannot afford to move into the neighborhood and pay an expensive mortgage, which now essentially has become the cost of private school tuition.

Whatever you think about public schools, the wealth disparity between districts seems to contradict the primary purpose of providing equal access to high quality education to *all*—especially for those who can't afford it. With that in mind, consider economist Milton Friedman's insights into the four ways money can be spent, and the likely outcomes of each.

1. **Spending your own money on yourself:** Here, you are most likely to be careful and choose only the best value. Poor decisions are borne entirely by you on both the spending and receiving side.

2. **Spending someone else's money on yourself:** There is a little less incentive to be careful, but since you live with the result, there is still an eye for value. You bear part of the cost of the decision, the receiving side.

3. **Spending your own money on someone else:** Yes, it's your money, but the other person lives with the result, so you're less scrupulous here than when buying for yourself. Again, you bear part of the cost of the decision, the spending side.

4. **Spending someone else's money on someone else:** The least accountability to value. You don't have a strong incentive to be thrifty or look for high quality. Nothing bad happens to you if you spend poorly, as you bear no cost on the spending or receiving side.

The idea of public education rules out option 1, as the primary purpose is to provide public resources (via tax dollars) equally to all, especially to those who can't afford it or don't have access to the resources they need (i.e., a quality education). Ideally, option 2 is the best of all because it combines public funding with personal stake in the outcome. When parents can use public education dollars to choose their children's schools (through scholarship accounts, vouchers, or similar programs), they remain highly motivated to make good choices since their children's future depends on it, while still benefiting from public support to access better options. Option 3 represents traditional private school scholarships or philanthropy in education, where wealthy donors or foundations fund others' education. While this can provide opportunities for some students, the donors may focus on their own priorities or preferences rather than what recipients need most, and there is less accountability for educational outcomes than when parents are directly involved. And option 4 should be avoided at all costs because it creates a system where decision makers bear no direct consequences for either poor spending choices or poor educational outcomes. Without skin in the game on either side, there is little incentive to maximize value or ensure quality, leading to inefficient use of resources and low educational achievement.

The public school system represents the fourth type of spending, and any attempts to make it more efficient and accountable do nothing to fix these poor underlying incentives. The experts brought in to come up with accountability metrics are themselves in the fourth position. They're spending other people's money (taxpayer dollars) to create systems that affect other people's children. They do not directly pay for the implementation of their metrics, nor do their own children necessarily attend the schools they're evaluating. Without personal stakes in either the costs or outcomes, these experts lack the incentives to create truly effective accountability systems. No amount of centralized spending control or bureaucratic oversight can match the effectiveness of

> *Parents are the ultimate accountability system.*

allowing parents and students to make direct decisions about their educational resources and options. As the former Secretary of Education, Betsy DeVos, once said, "Parents are the ultimate accountability system."

The Launch (and Failure) of "No Child Left Behind"

In 2000, due to the disparity in educational outcomes among students across the country, plus the continued reports of the U.S. falling behind other countries in test scores, the ultra-conservative Senator Orrin Hatch of Utah and the ultra-liberal Sen. Ted Kennedy of Massachusetts worked together to bridge the political divide. The following year, a massive, bi-partisan federal law, called "No Child Left Behind" (NCLB), was passed with overwhelming support from both political parties. Among other things, the law required that in the subsequent 12 years, every state needed to achieve **100%** student proficiency in math and reading in order to continue receiving billions of dollars in federal funding. The implementation of NCLB revealed a deeper problem in education policy. By setting an impossible target of 100% proficiency in math and reading, the legislation created a system designed to document failure rather than promote success. Both political parties supported this framework despite its unattainable goals, likely because it provided leverage for their respective education reform agendas. Democrats could argue for increased funding to help schools meet these standards, while Republicans could use falling test scores to advocate for private sector alternatives.

The impact on classroom teaching was profound. The obsession over test scores from NCLB destroyed the joy that many teachers felt about their career. Instead of fostering deeper learning through creative teaching methods, educators found themselves constrained by test-preparation curricula designed to raise scores rather than promote understanding. This shift not only affected teacher morale but also transformed the role of educators from mentors and guides into what many came to describe as babysitting test-preppers. The focus on test scores overshadowed other vital aspects of education that motivate both students and teachers, such as comprehension, critical thinking, and the natural joy of discovery.

The consequences of test-focused education extend far beyond academic metrics. The obsession with standardized testing has stripped a generation of children of vital developmental experiences and time for arts, social sciences, music, and crucially, unstructured play. Many children, overwhelmed by the rigid structure and academic pressure of the school day, began to seek refuge in screens during their free time. Today, what we often label as iPad addiction might actually be a symptom of an education system that has stripped away natural outlets for creativity and relaxation. After spending hours in highly structured, test-focused environments where spontaneity and natural learning rhythms are suppressed, children often turn to screens not out of mere habit, but as a form of mental decompression. This mirrors what many adults experience after intense workdays—gravitating toward entertainment media as a low-effort way to recover from cognitive fatigue. Research has shown that individuals experiencing mental exhaustion (or ego depletion) are more likely to use media for stress recovery, even though feelings of guilt may reduce its effectiveness.[1]

For children, whose developing brains are especially sensitive to stress and overstimulation, the need for downtime is even more acute. The more packed a child's school days are with test preparation and rigid academic structures, the more they seek mindless entertainment as a form of relief. Sadly, many traditional schools use recess as a reward for good behavior and force misbehaving students to miss recess and instead sit quietly to learn how to behave. This is the opposite of what that child needs. Children need to move their bodies frequently and benefit greatly from becoming physically exhausted before being mentally ready to learn. A parent once commented that her young daughter was extremely social and would talk a lot in class. As a result, her teacher would punish her daughter by not allowing her to go to recess; yet recess was the very outlet she needed to address her yearning to be social with friends so she could successfully focus on learning during class time.

After two decades of NCLB's failure, both major political parties continue to weaponize test scores to advance their preferred solutions. Rather than question the validity of standardized testing as the primary measure of educational success, lawmakers use poor test results to justify their existing policy preferences, whether that is increasing funding or promoting privatization.

This approach has not only failed to improve education, it has actually contributed to *declining test scores* which have led some states to simply lower their standards rather than address the underlying issues.[2] The real tragedy is that this system not only fails to measure what matters in education—creativity, continuous progress, critical thinking, skill development, and more—it actively works against it. While politicians and policymakers debate solutions based on test scores, the fundamental needs of children to move, play, socially interact, and experience genuine discovery continue to be sacrificed. This disconnect demonstrates the system's own failure to understand how children actually learn and develop.

It's Easy to Predict Test Scores

Predicting a school's test scores is so easy that an entry-level statistician could do it with a high degree of accuracy without ever looking at actual scores. What method would they use to predict high test scores? Would they use the per-pupil state spending? No. Just do a quick comparison of Utah with New York. Utah spends approximately $10,000 per student to get average test scores, whereas New York spends about $35,000 per student and gets below average test scores.[3] Maybe the statistician would use factors such as teacher credentials, teacher experience, school class size, instructional methodology, or curriculum choice to predict success on state tests. Would that help? Nope. None of those factors matter when it comes to actual test scores. In fact, there is only one data point which matters, and it has for nearly two hundred years: **household income**.

According to analysis from the Penn Wharton Budget Model, household income shows a consistently positive correlation with standardized test performance across all major assessments.[4] For instance, SAT math and ACT composite scores each have a correlation of about 0.22 to 0.23 with household income—roughly three times stronger than the relationship between income and school-specific metrics like GPA or class rank. In other words, students from higher-income families tend to score higher on national standardized exams, not necessarily because they've learned more in school, but because these exams also capture access to resources and opportunities outside the classroom.

In short, standardized test scores don't reflect the learning that happens *inside* a classroom. They more accurately reflect the student's access to learning experiences *outside* the classroom. Under the guise of "public accountability," parents, teachers, and community leaders have been convinced that a child's learning is measurable by a standardized test. In reality, that assumption is blatantly false. This highly lauded but misguided testing mechanism simply measures the amount of overall access a student has with engaging activities above and beyond the classroom. Therefore, standardized test scores have very little to do with a child's actual schooling experience. This is where you, as a parent, come in. For over a hundred years, it has been culturally acceptable in society for parents to simply send their child to their boundary district

> *Standardized test scores don't reflect the learning that happens inside a classroom. They more accurately reflect the student's access to learning experiences outside the classroom.*

school and expect the child to receive a quality education worthy of future success. No one judged them for that. And a grandma and grandpa or aunt and uncle at a family gathering won't blame a parent for doing that.

Times are different now.

The Post-COVID Awakening

The growing resistance to standardized testing became impossible to ignore in the years following the COVID-19 pandemic. When more than 200,000 New York parents opted their children out of end-of-year testing in 2022, they sent a clear message about the toll that testing was taking on their children's education.[5] This wasn't just isolated pushback, it was part of a broader shift in how families approached traditional education. In the wake of the COVID-19 pandemic, public school enrollment dropped by 1.2 million students across 37 states, affecting two-thirds of school districts nationwide.[6]

The reasons for this shift are complex. As Stanford University researcher Thomas Dee has documented, the COVID-era enrollment declines were due to a combination of factors, including a rise in homeschooling, a shift to private schools, fewer school-age children, and some students who simply went missing from the data.[7] But the story doesn't end there. Once parents got a taste of alternatives during the pandemic, many started to question the status quo. They began to explore options beyond the traditional public school system, seeking educational approaches that better fit their children's needs and their family's values.

Once parents got a taste of alternatives during the pandemic, many started to question the status quo.

Education researcher and author Michael B. Horn describes this shift as part of a larger trend toward the unbundling of education. In his work, Horn argues that we are seeing a gradual move away from the one-size-fits-all model of schooling toward more personalized, à la carte educational options.[8] However, he cautions that this change isn't happening overnight. Yet, on a one-hundred-year timescale, this transformation is happening at a remarkable pace. The rigid, industrial model of education that has dominated for more than a century is showing signs of cracking, and alternatives are gaining traction faster than many anticipated. Still, there are significant transaction costs associated with piecing together a customized, open education plan, which can make the process daunting for many families. For many parents, it seems the only viable option is simply to drop their kids off at school from 8:30 a.m. to 3:00 p.m. every weekday during the school year (and figure out plans for the rest of the year when school is not in session), so they can work and support their family.

Since the global COVID-19 pandemic, parents at various income levels have been presented with more flexible, remote work environments. At the same time, families have experienced continuously expanding remote learning opportunities for children and young adults. Still, many parents are reluctant to engage in different education options for fear of being ridiculed, ostracized, rejected, or labeled as a bad parent. The weight of tradition and societal expectations can be heavy, and stepping outside the norm often requires courage and conviction.

Thankfully, it is becoming more culturally acceptable to intentionally choose what is best for your child when it comes to their education. In fact, the public sentiment is beginning to shift, and parents are often now openly apologizing for not taking a more active role in their child's education. This shift does not mean the end for public schools, but it does signal a need for adaptation. As families increasingly seek educational options that align with their values and their children's needs, schools and policymakers must evolve to meet these changing demands.

The stigma around alternative education approaches is fading. What was once seen as fringe or unconventional is becoming more mainstream. Parents who choose to homeschool, enroll in online or hybrid programs, or are actively designing their own open education plan, are finding more validation and resources than ever before.

The Homeschool Pioneers of Open Education

For most of history before the public school era, kids generally learned at home. This was the norm. But when compulsory public education became widespread, the concept of learning at home in a familiar environment coupled with regular playtime and community support was forgotten. There was a sort of cultural amnesia about the fact that kids can learn at home, and had for thousands of years.

As early as the 1960s, pioneering parents rediscovered learning at home, and the modern concept of homeschooling emerged. It was mostly illegal until a push by the growing homeschool community throughout the 1980s resulted in court victories and policy changes. Before that time, the only school choice presented to parents for a century was either a "free" public school or an expensive private school (if you could afford it). Even then, homeschooling was viewed as a rare, fringe thing for families to choose.

In the early 1980s, it's estimated that there were between 60,000 and 125,000 homeschool students in the U.S.[9] It was a small, dedicated, and fast-growing movement. Parents created networks, newsletters, co-ops, sports leagues, extra-curricular clubs, conferences, and publishing houses for curricula. The 1990s saw homeschooling grow from 250,000 students at the start of the decade to over 1 million by the end. Tracking the actual number of homeschool students remains difficult, and the numbers are often dubious, but there are around 3.5 million homeschooled students in the U.S. today.[10] Remember that drop of over 1 million enrollments from public school since COVID-19? Homeschooling grew by about 1 million during that same period.

Early homeschoolers paved the way for the open education movement of today. These brave parents had to forge their own path, often with little to no support or resources except what they could create themselves. They were the radicals. They showed a different way was possible.

When Isaac was a kid, people would find out he was homeschooled, wrinkle their faces, and say to his mother, "Aren't you worried about social skills?" Today, the most common response when people find out we homeschool our children is, "Oh cool! I wish I could do that." What society considers acceptable—what political scientists call The Overton Window—has shifted dramatically on this issue, and people are increasingly open to educational options beyond traditional schooling. Thankfully, the landscape of homeschooling has evolved dramatically since those early days.

The technological and social changes of the past few decades, and especially since 2020, have opened up possibilities that didn't exist for early homeschoolers. These families were fighting for the legal right to not be forced to attend public schools, even though they were still forced to pay for them with their taxes. They did not have the option to pick and choose sports, activities, or elements of public (or private) school that they might want, and discard the rest. It was an all-or-nothing deal. You either sent your kid to school and did everything their way, or pulled your kid out and did everything alone.

Now, the option set has exploded. What it means to be homeschooled is different today than what it once did. Of course, parents may choose to teach their kids fully at home and not engage with any other options, schools, programs, or providers. But if they want to, they can choose to involve those other offerings in their education. That choice wasn't there before.

Sometimes people ask, "Isn't open education just another name for homeschooling?" Yes and no. Homeschoolers are open educators, to be sure. They are crafting an experience for their children. But not all open educators are homeschoolers. You might create a combination of private and public classes, books, experiences, and activities that don't look quite like traditional homeschooling or public schooling. The open education mindset is about thinking beyond the labels.

The goal is not to replace the current one-size-fits-all system with an alternative one-size fits all solution. Nor is the goal to exit or defund traditional public schools that still serve a crucial need for millions of families. Rather, the objective is to help more parents recognize that the world is opening up, in some areas quickly, in some areas slowly. The demand for more flexible, responsive education is already changing the landscape in ways that better serve the unique needs and potential of each child. Our collective task is to embrace that change and accelerate it for those who are ready to take that next step.

The two-hundred-year-old trap of standardized education is losing its grip, and this raises urgent questions that every parent must confront. How do we know when the public system is no longer serving our children? What are we really measuring when we measure student success? What becomes possible when we stop trying to standardize children and start embracing their unique potential? The answers might surprise you.

To understand these possibilities, we first need to confront an uncomfortable truth about how our education system views students—and why that view is holding back not just the exceptional few, but every child who has ever felt that school could be something more.

CHAPTER 1 RECAP:

- The current public school system is based on an outdated, two-year-old model built for turning the kids into good factory workers.
- Wealthy families avoided the public school system in favor of highly-customized, private education models for their children.
- Children were sorted into birth-year cohorts and were graded like meat on an assembly line.
- The nation's bi-partisan obsession with using standardized testing to "hold schools accountable" turned teachers into "test-preppers" and destroyed the creativity of a generation of kids. Parents are the ultimate accountability system.
- Standardized test scores don't reflect the learning that happens *inside* a classroom. They more accurately reflect the student's access to learning experiences *outside* the classroom.
- The COVID-19 pandemic awakened parents to think differently about their child's schooling and millions are now taking a more open approach to education.

CHAPTER 2:

STUDENTS ARE NOT STANDARD

— For a fair final exam, everyone must climb the tree. —

Can Fish Climb Trees?

Would you ask a fish to climb a tree? A penguin to fly? An elephant to swing from branches? Of course not. Yet, every day, the traditional education system subjects children with vastly different talents, interests, and ways of thinking to this kind of absurdity. Students are all put through the same standardized tests, measured against the same arbitrary benchmarks, and then labeled as failures if they do not meet the standards. The tragedy isn't just that this approach fails to recognize individual differences among students; the real tragedy is that this approach actively punishes them.

Everybody wants a piece of Albert Einstein's legacy of genius. Schools name their gifted programs after him. Companies stamp his wild-haired face on their motivational posters. His name has become shorthand for brilliance itself. The irony is that Einstein's genius emerged in spite of the education system, not because of it.

The man who revolutionized our understanding of the universe was labeled a poor student, failed his college entrance exams, and struggled to speak until age nine. Yet, he went on to win the Nobel Prize and change our very understanding of reality itself. The quote shown in the image is often attributed to Einstein, which perfectly captures this irony:

"Everybody is a genius. But if you judge a fish by its ability to climb a tree, it will live its whole life believing that it is stupid."

Like many of the most famous Einstein quotes, he likely never actually said this; though, in keeping with our unshakeable human need to connect wisdom to Einstein, we're quoting it anyway. In truth, the line appears to have originated with an 1898 essay by physicist Amos E. Dolbear of Tufts University, who wrote a clever allegory about animals being forced through a standardized school system. But perhaps it is fitting that we want Einstein to have said it; after all, who better to critique our education system than history's most famous struggling student?

The story of Einstein's early schooling illustrates a truth that parents and educators are finally beginning to acknowledge.

Our system of standardized testing and rigid assessment is not identifying aptitudes nor helping students learn. Instead, it is breaking our children. It is creating unprecedented levels of anxiety, depression, and alienation. It is crushing curiosity and creativity. And perhaps most tragically, it is teaching young people that their worth can be reduced to a number on a test.

The problem isn't that adults want to measure student learning; the problem is that tests are measuring the wrong things in the wrong ways. The writer and humorist William Bruce Cameron once observed, "Not everything that can be counted counts, and not everything that counts can be counted." Like the fish-climbing-trees quote, this quote is also often mistakenly attributed to Einstein, perhaps because we desperately want someone with Einstein's scientific authority to validate what we know intuitively about human potential. An entire system has been built around quantifying and standardizing things that, by their very nature, resist standardization. The result is that we end up valuing what we can measure, rather than creatively measuring what we truly value.

A brilliant young musician might struggle with algebra. A gifted programmer might have trouble with essay writing. A natural entrepreneur might find themselves bored to tears in a traditional economics class. These aren't failures of the students; they're failures of a system that insists on measuring everyone with the same rigid yardstick. Recent research underscores just how damaging this one-size-fits-all approach can be. A 2021 study in the journal of *Education Finance and Policy* found that during high-stakes testing weeks, students' stress hormone levels spike by an average of 15% compared to normal school weeks.[11] For some students, particularly boys and those from high-poverty neighborhoods, this increase can reach as high as 35%.

> *These aren't failures of the students; they're failures of a system that insists on measuring everyone with the same rigid yardstick.*

In other words, our testing regime isn't merely ineffective, it's creating trauma.

Behind these statistics are real children sitting in real classrooms with hearts racing as they stare at test booklets that will supposedly determine their future. Picture the 3rd grader who used to love reading until it became something to be constantly tested, or the middle schooler who now gets stomach aches every Sunday night, or the high school student who has learned to equate their self-worth with their SAT score. These are not mere anecdotes. These stories reflect the human cost of a system that values standardization over individual potential.

Meeting Standardized Testing Head On

Defenders of standardized testing argue that objective measures are needed to ensure accountability. They ask what other methods show if students are learning, if schools are performing, and if tax dollars are being well spent. These are reasonable questions. But they rest on a misunderstanding of a) how humans learn, b) what kind of learning actually matters in the modern world, and c) who is best positioned to determine whether an education is working. Let's confront these questions directly.

When advocates for standardized testing talk about accountability, what are they really trying to measure? And for whom?

Consider how assessment works in other areas of life. When a young athlete is developing, they are not given a single high-stakes test to determine their future. Instead, their progress is observed over time, their improvements are celebrated, and their skills develop at different rates. When a musician learns, instructors assess their growing mastery of various techniques, their ability to interpret pieces, their stage presence, and their collaboration with others. In education, however, the traditional system clings to standardized tests as the only way to measure learning. As many frustrated teachers are discovering, artificial intelligence models can now easily complete and pass these rote tests. As a middle school student recently remarked to her teacher, "If AI can answer it, maybe you shouldn't have asked it on your test." That may not always be true, but she understands the heart of something that many adults seem to have forgotten. Real education should focus on developing uniquely human capabilities like creativity, critical thinking, emotional intelligence, and the ability to solve novel problems.

The irony is that even as the traditional education system clings to standardized testing in schools, the world beyond education is moving in the opposite direction. Major companies like Google, Apple, and IBM have dropped degree requirements for many positions, focusing instead on demonstrated skills and capabilities. Leading universities are increasingly going test-optional, recognizing that SAT and ACT scores are poor predictors of college success. Even traditional professions like law and medicine are rethinking their reliance on standardized testing, with many law schools now accepting GRE instead of LSAT scores.

So, why persist with a system that the real world is increasingly rejecting? The answer lies partly in institutional inertia, partly in the testing industry's enormous financial interests, and partly in a fundamental misunderstanding of how humans actually learn. Consider what employers really want. When surveyed about essential skills for the modern workforce, they rank creativity, problem-solving, collaboration, and adaptability at the top of their lists.[12] None of these can be measured through standardized tests. The testing regime ignores these very capabilities. No wonder employers are ignoring grades and test scores.

When Isaac was young, his mom insisted he do a software program called "Mavis Beacon Teaches Typing." He never put his hands and fingers in the right place on the keyboard. Instead, he typed with only his two index fingers. He failed the typing technique test miserably. If testing is really useful, that experience should indicate that he would not be successful with work that involved typing. To this day, he types with two fingers. (He typed this very sentence with two fingers.) He loves to type. He has written over 3,000 articles, written or ghost-written twelve books, and has little trouble with speed or accuracy in typing. Add the presence of touchscreens and voice-to-text, and those old typing tests seem even less useful.

This disconnect between traditional grading scales and real-world success is not lost on today's students. Whether they're aspiring athletes, dancers, chess players, or e-sports enthusiasts, they can see that making half your shots or winning just over half your points can make you a star, not a failure. This brings us to perhaps the most absurd aspect of standardized testing. These types of rigid tests demand behaviors that would be considered counterproductive or even unethical in any real-world situation. When faced with a problem to solve, test-takers must not collaborate with others, must not research additional information, must work under artificial time pressure, and get only one shot to arrive at the right answer, with no possibility of fixing or re-doing it if they get it wrong. In what real-world scenario would this approach make sense?

> *This disconnect between traditional grading scales and real-world success is not lost on today's students.*

The truth about standardized testing is even more troubling when we examine what it actually measures. As mentioned earlier, decades of research have shown that test scores correlate more strongly with socioeconomic status than with classroom learning.[13] Even the test design itself can be deliberately misleading. Matt discovered this firsthand in college while practicing a 1st grade reading assessment with a fellow student. Following the exact instructions led his college-educated peer to fail a test meant for six-year-olds, not because she couldn't read, but because the unclear instructions deliberately misdirected her attention. When a college graduate can fail a 1st grade reading test, you have to wonder what we're really measuring with standardized tests.

Standardized tests do not measure public schools, they measure a student's socioeconomic privilege, access to outside support and resources, motivation, test-taking skills, and the ability to navigate hidden expectations. These flawed metrics are used to make life-altering decisions about students' futures.

Of course we need accountability in education. But there should also be some clarity about what we're actually trying to measure and why. Right now, American schools spend an estimated $1.7 billion annually on standardized testing, and that's just the direct costs. Factor in the instructional time lost to test prep, the narrowing of curriculum, the disruption to family life and schedule, and the psychological toll on students, and the true price becomes staggering. Meanwhile, these tests reveal remarkably little about whether students are developing the skills they will actually need in life.

The Myth of Standardization as Rigor

When people defend standardized testing, they often conflate standardization with rigor. They assume that if everyone takes the same test under the same conditions, high standards are maintained. But this fundamentally misrepresents what real rigor looks like.

In fields from athletics to the arts, from entrepreneurship to scientific research, mastery develops through a different process, one of feedback, practice, and critique. A scientist, for example, builds on previous experiments, collaborates with colleagues, submits to peer review, and revises hypotheses based on new data and arguments. As education researcher Peter Gray has documented in his studies of self-directed learning, children naturally tackle complex challenges when given the freedom to explore their interests[14]. At the Sudbury Valley School (SVS), where students direct their own learning without standardized curriculum or testing, nearly 90% of graduates go on to higher education, with most getting into their first-choice colleges.

Compared to the general population, SVS graduates are more likely to work in management positions, technology careers, education, and helping professions. Many become entrepreneurs.[15] The key is that these students haven't just memorized facts, they've learned how to learn. They have developed personal responsibility, initiative, and the ability to tackle new challenges with confidence.

Yet, traditional education has somehow convinced parents and teachers that real rigor means sitting alone with a test booklet and racing against a clock, with no access to resources or collaboration. This standardized approach isn't just artificial, it actively prevents the kind of deep learning that true rigor requires. When teachers are pressured to teach to the test, they can't foster the kind of rich, open-ended exploration that leads to genuine understanding. When students know they will be judged solely on test performance, they learn to prioritize memorization over comprehension, compliance over creativity.

The belief that meaningful measurement requires uniformity ignores how assessment works in virtually every other field. A chef's skill isn't measured by a multiple choice test about cooking; it is demonstrated through the food they create. A programmer's ability isn't determined by standardized coding questions, it's proven through the applications they build. A researcher's impact isn't evaluated through timed exams, it's shown through their contributions to their field. In each case, excellence is measured through authentic demonstration of skills in context. The standards are high, but the paths to meet them are diverse. This is true rigor, which is quite unlike the artificial uniformity of standardized testing.

Yes, students who perform well on standardized tests often succeed in college and careers. Researchers have consistently found correlations between test scores and later outcomes like educational attainment and employment. But this correlation reveals less than it seems. Consider that children from wealthy families tend to score better on standardized tests. They also tend to have better access to college and career opportunities. Their test scores don't predict their success; their socioeconomic advantages predict both. It's a classic case of correlation being confused with causation. More telling are the success stories that defy the testing narrative. For example, the Sudbury Valley School graduates who excel in college despite never taking a standardized test; the entrepreneurs who struggled with traditional academics but build thriving businesses; the late bloomers who find their path after leaving the constraints of conventional schooling. These examples remind us that human potential cannot be reduced to a number. When test scores are mistaken for destiny, opportunities become limited for students who might thrive given different ways to demonstrate their capabilities.

Similarly, the outdated school system has uncovered a peculiar, illogical belief. It assumes that all children should learn everything at the same rate and age, regardless of their inherent differences and experiences. This idea is at odds with everything we know about human development.

If you have more than one child, you have already seen how differently children develop. One child might walk at eight months, while another takes their first steps at 18 months. One might show an early facility with numbers, while another excels in language skills. A third might struggle with reading until age 10, then accelerate past their peers. Would one child be viewed as smarter or more advanced than the other? Would one be seen as less capable or destined for failure? Of course not. Yet, our education system, born from the industrial revolution, treats these differences as problems to be solved rather than realities to be embraced.

The birth-year cohort model—grouping children strictly by age—emerged less from any understanding of how children learn than from the need to process large numbers of students efficiently, like products on an assembly line. It was designed for administrative convenience, not for educational effectiveness. This factory model made some sense in the 1800s when Horace Mann convinced American industry executives that the Prussian system of education could produce obedient workers for their factories. Remember that the goal of this system was standardization, creating predictable, uniform outputs (soldiers/workers). Students were divided into cohorts by birth year and zip code, without any consideration of their individual needs, interests, or developmental pace. Today, this approach persists despite mounting evidence of its failures.

Modern science teaches that brain development varies significantly among children. Interest and motivation play crucial roles in learning. Different learning styles and special needs require different approaches and timelines. Yet, the traditional education model expects every eight-year-old to read at the same level, every 12-year-old to grasp algebra at the same pace, and every teenager to master complex concepts on the same schedule. Consider how this plays out in schools. Teachers, knowing they must move all students through the curriculum at the same rate, face an impossible choice. If they move too quickly, struggling students fall behind. If they move too slowly, advanced students become bored and disengaged. The result? In trying to teach everyone at the same pace, teachers end up targeting a mythical "average" student who doesn't actually exist.

When children don't progress at the standardized pace, protectors of the system too often view this as a failure of the child rather than a failure of the system itself. A student who learns differently becomes a problem to solve rather than a unique individual to nurture. This mindset transforms schools from what they should be—active, exciting discovery centers that inspire a lifelong love of learning—into something more akin to sterile hospitals. Teachers are forced to diagnose problems through assessment data, issue treatments via worksheets, monitor progress through homework, and determine whether the patient (i.e., student) can be issued a

> *In trying to teach everyone at the same pace, teachers end up targeting a mythical "average" student who doesn't actually exist.*

clean bill of health by passing a standardized test. The absurdity of this approach becomes even more clear in our technological age.

While the world races forward with AI and other advances, schools cling to industrial-age methods. Just as previous generations of educators fought losing battles against calculators in math class, today's system often resists rather than embraces new tools that could help personalize learning. Instead of leveraging technology to allow students to learn at their own pace, they are forced to power down their devices and conform to the same uniform schedule. This resistance to change reveals something fundamental about our education system. It was never designed for learning; it was designed for processing diverse groups of students and standardizing them into uniform outputs. This raises an uncomfortable question. Who is the education system actually serving?

The Student as a Product

Without standardized tests, parents and teachers might wonder how to measure a child's progress to know when they are ready to move forward. Ironically, nearly all students advance to the next grade and eventually graduate regardless of whether they've mastered the material. The system doesn't actually care about learning, it cares about processing. If a student gets labeled as "D-grade," they aren't sent back for improvement, they're simply moved along the conveyor belt with their new inferior-quality label attached. The district's hands are clean because they assessed the student, found them wanting, and informed the parents. The conveyor belt keeps running.

Follow the money and you will see who this system really serves. As of 2025, U.S. student loan borrowers collectively owe $1.77 trillion in federal and private student loan debt.[16] Universities spend billions marketing to and recruiting students who have been properly processed by the K-12 system. The U.S. test preparation market is projected to grow by $16.28 billion from

2023 to 2028.[17] This massive financial engine shapes everything about how society approaches education. In K-12 public education, students aren't actually the customers at all, they are the product! Instead of children learning life skills and developing their natural gifts, they are trained to progress from being student products to higher education products and finally to employee products. Each transition demands some kind of external validation metrics, even if they have little to do with growth and fulfillment. The true customers are college admissions offices and corporate HR departments, or worse yet, government bureaucrats who have been allowed to dictate the terms of what education should look like.

> *In K-12 public education, students aren't actually the customers at all, they are the product!*

This manufacturing mindset has created a self-perpetuating cycle. When teachers are evaluated based on test scores, they are forced to prioritize test prep over authentic learning. When the curriculum is designed to satisfy college admissions requirements rather than spark curiosity and develop real-world capabilities, countless opportunities for meaningful education are lost. When students are treated as products to be processed rather than minds to be developed, it's no wonder they become disengaged from learning altogether.

The Education Transparency Problem

There is something fundamentally broken about a system that hides its assessment criteria from students, parents, and even teachers. Under the rationale of ensuring testing fidelity, standardized test vendors insist that all test questions must remain secret. This creates a bizarre situation where students are expected to prove their knowledge without telling them what they need to know or how they will be evaluated.

Consider the various aspects of life where performance and knowledge are judged. Most often, you know the judging criteria before undertaking the effort. Imagine trying to get a driver's license if the DMV wouldn't let you review traffic rules before the test. Or a builder being denied access to construction codes before inspection. Olympic athletes must know exactly how their performances will be judged before they perform. No one would expect a gymnast to practice for years with a coach who doesn't know the scoring system, then perform in front of judges without understanding the criteria. Military service members understand precisely what they need to demonstrate for promotion.

Critics of educational transparency often say, "Would you like to be operated on by a doctor who knew the test questions?" But this misses the point entirely. Would you rather have a doctor who has demonstrated expertise through hands-on practical experience, or one who simply memorized answers to hidden test questions? Yet, the current education system deliberately hides assessment criteria from those who need to know it prior to the assessment. These hidden tests are literally making children sick with stress. Teachers must guess what might be tested, leading to scattered test prep rather than coherent instruction. Students learn to fear assessment rather than see it as a tool for growth. Parents are left in the dark about how to help their children improve.

This obsession with secrecy serves no educational purpose. Its only beneficiaries are the testing companies themselves, who can avoid scrutiny of their questions while maintaining their position as gatekeepers of educational advancement. In any meaningful learning experience, students should understand what success looks like. They should know what they are aiming for and receive clear feedback about how to improve. Instead, the testing regime treats assessment like a game of gotcha, where success depends on correctly guessing what anonymous test creators think is important (and which is most often learned outside the classroom anyway).

Parents see the damage this does. A child who loves reading for the sake of reading becomes anxious about reading comprehension tests. A student who excels at mathematical thinking starts to doubt their abilities because they can't decode what the test questions are really asking. Teachers report spending weeks teaching students how to think like the test maker rather than actually deepening their understanding of the subject matter.

To anyone who still doubts the barrier posed to real education by teaching to the test, we return to the man so universally revered for his creative genius. While Einstein never said the majority of clever things attributed to him, what he *did* say speaks volumes:

> School failed me, and I failed the school. It bored me. The teachers behaved like sergeants. I wanted to learn what I wanted to know, but they wanted me to learn for the exam . . . I felt that my thirst for knowledge was being strangled by my teachers; grades were their only measurement. How can a teacher understand youth with such a system?[18]

Ironically, Einstein was speaking about his experience in late 1800s Germany, the very birthplace of the standardized education model adopted in the U.S. He lived under the epitome of the Prussian system, with its rigid hierarchies, strict discipline, and relentless focus on conformity. While Germany eventually evolved its approach, creating different educational tracts to accommodate various aptitudes and career paths, the U.S. imported the worst aspects of the Prussian model and then refused to let it evolve.

A century and a half later, American students still face essentially the same system that frustrated young Einstein. And now we have added a cruel new twist. Rather than acknowledging different paths for different talents, we force every student through the same narrow academic tunnel, where their future hangs on their grades in a standardized curriculum. These grades become a brand that follows them for life, determining college admission, career opportunities, and even self-worth.

The price of this obsession extends far beyond the money spent annually on standardized testing. When schools become test-prep centers rather than places of discovery, when teachers are forced to act like Einstein's "sergeants" rather than guides and mentors, children lose the natural love of learning they all bring to their first day of school.

The world needs innovators and problem-solvers who can tackle complex issues. Instead, the system is producing students who have learned to seek the right answer rather than think critically, who avoid risk rather than embrace challenge. Einstein's thirst for knowledge was nearly strangled by this system. How many modern-day Einsteins are we losing to these same practices?

> *Learning happens differently for each student, at different paces, and in different ways and places.*

There *is* a better way. Just as Einstein argued that grades shouldn't be the only measurement, our education system needs to evolve and recognize that learning happens differently for each student, at different paces, and in different ways and places. But before a reimagined model of growth and learning can exist, we need to understand how our obsession with grades has trapped us in a system that confuses measurement with meaning.

CHAPTER 2 RECAP:

- Every child is unique. There's no such thing as an "average" child.
- "If you judge a fish by its ability to climb a tree, it will live its whole life believing that it is stupid."
- Major companies like Google, Apple, and IBM have dropped a formal college degree requirement for many positions, focusing instead on demonstrated skills and capabilities.

- Leading universities are increasingly going test-optional, recognizing that SAT and ACT scores are poor predictors of college success.

- Sadly, children are viewed as the "product," not the customer, which primarily benefits post-secondary institutions and corporations.

- When people defend standardized testing, they often conflate standardization with rigor.

- There is something fundamentally broken about a system that hides its assessment criteria from students, parents, and even teachers. We all must demand more educational transparency.

- The outdated school system's belief that all children should learn everything at the same rate and age is at odds with everything we know about human development.

- The world needs innovators and problem solvers who can tackle complex issues.

CHAPTER 3:

"MASTERED" OR "NOT YET?"

L eBron James is a failure... at least, he would be if we were to grade him like we grade our kids. Let's look at his report card:

Subject	Percentage / Grade
Field goal percentage	50% (F)
3-point field goal percentage	35% (F)
Free throw percentage	73% (D+)
Regular season winning percentage	66% (D-)
Playoff winning percentage	65% (D-)
Finals winning percentage	40% (F)
Overall Grade Average	**55% (F)**

By academic standards, the man widely considered one of the greatest basketball players of all time would be on academic probation. And he's not alone. Roger Federer, arguably one of the most talented tennis players ever to grace a court, won an impressive 80% (B-) of his matches but only 54% of the points he played, barely better than a coin flip. Again, F.

Simone Biles, the most decorated gymnast in history, has won medals in "only" 61% of her Olympic events. In school terms, she's lucky to eke out a D-. Baseball is even more extreme. The greatest hitters get out roughly twice as often as they make it on base. They would also get an F grade.

Something is wrong with this picture.

Imagine if coaches told these athletes they were failures because they didn't score 90% of the time. Imagine if children were held to standards that would label Michael Jordan, with a career shooting percentage of 49.7%, a failure. Yet, every day, in classrooms across the country, this very thing happens. The education system takes young minds as unique and varied as Federer's serve, Biles's floor routine, and James's court vision, and reduces them to a crude letter grade that often means nothing.

The problem isn't just that the grading system is too harsh, it's that the system of measurement fundamentally misunderstands how humans learn, grow, and achieve mastery. This system is so obsessed with sorting and labeling that many of those entrenched in it have forgotten what education is actually meant to offer.

Consider what these athletes' careers demonstrate about learning and achievement:

- Success isn't about never failing, it's about how you respond to failure.
- Mastery comes through iteration and improvement, not one-time performance.
- Different skills develop at different rates.
- The path to excellence isn't linear. Progress happens in fits and starts.

Yet, our education system, with its rigid grading scales and K-12 birth-year cohorts, pretends none of this is true. This system acts as if learning happens in neat, predictable increments, identical for every child. Worst of all, the system makes children afraid to take the kinds of risks that lead to real learning.

Rethinking What Mastery Means

Imagine telling LeBron James that his missed shots in practice don't count toward improvement. That each game is a one-and-done test, with no chance to learn from mistakes. That he needs to master dribbling, shooting, and defense all at the same exact pace as every other player born in 1984.

Watch any great athlete train and you will see the same pattern: attempt, fail, adjust, try again. When Stephen Curry practices his legendary three-point shot, he's not aiming for a perfect score; he's seeking constant improvement. Some days he might hit 80% of his shots, other days only 30%. But each attempt, whether successful or not, builds toward mastery.

> *Watch any great athlete train and you will see the same pattern: attempt, fail, adjust, try again.*

Musicians understand this intuitively. No one expects a violinist to perfect a piece in one sitting. They practice sections repeatedly, sometimes spending hours on a single measure. They record themselves, get feedback from teachers, and gradually piece everything together. The final performance isn't a test, it's a demonstration of accumulated mastery. Likewise, scientists build their careers on failure. Einstein didn't solve relativity in one afternoon. Each failed experiment provided data; each incorrect hypothesis pointed toward new possibilities. As Thomas Edison famously said, "I have not failed. I've just found 10,000 ways that won't work."

Unfortunately, our current education system assigns arbitrary letter grades (refer to the meat factory story) to children's progress primarily based on one-at-a-time test scores. Mastery doesn't work this way. Ask any successful coach and they will tell you that what matters isn't where you start, but how you progress. The question isn't "Did you get it right the first time?" but rather "Have you mastered it yet?"

A better way to think about learning is through competency-based education. This concept, already transforming lives in schools and programs daring to break free from the tyranny of meat-packing letter grades, is a simple but powerful idea. It's the "mastered" or "not yet" approach.

Take Matt's daughter, Eliza. At age 16, she was a capable student but found traditional schooling painfully rigid. After exploring different options, she enrolled in a competency-based program that used this "mastered" or "not yet" model. Instead of racing to keep pace with arbitrary deadlines, she could focus on truly mastering each concept before moving forward. She completed her associate degree in just 14 months, not because she rushed or the work wasn't rigorous, but because she could progress at her own pace, taking more time when she needed it and accelerating when she was ready. Since then, all five of Matt's children have earned one or more competency-based college degrees and have benefited greatly from the experience.

This philosophy of competency-based education is what drove Isaac to create the Praxis program, an alternative to college for entrepreneurial young adults. Rather than following traditional academic schedules and grading systems, Praxis offers an intensive 36-week professional development program that combines skill-building, mentorship, and real-world experience. When creating the program, Isaac used a very old mechanism for demonstrating competency that has been largely forgotten: oral exams. In addition to business principles and tech skills, the program had rigorous, self-guided modules on history, philosophy, and economics. When ready, participants had 30-minute oral exams with experts and authors in each field. Could they hold competent conversations? Could they engage the main ideas, debate, discuss, and explain? These were not mandatory but allowed participants to earn optional sections in their portfolio that showed "Excellent,"

"Complete," or "Incomplete" in each area. They could reschedule or retake these oral exams or use them just for personal discovery rather than to share with the world. Several of the examiners were also college professors, and they all raved about how enjoyable and engaging this experience was for them, compared to grading multiple-choice and essay tests.

This approach isn't about lowering standards; quite the opposite. In traditional schools, students routinely advance with Cs and Ds, moving forward without truly mastering the material. Remember the old saying that "Cs get degrees?" In competency-based education, a student either demonstrates mastery or keeps working. There is no settling for "close enough."

The Three Elements to Real Learning

Dr. Tanner Bowman (Matt's son), after years of research and earning a doctorate in education, identified something fascinating. His research demonstrated that true learning happens at the intersection of three critical elements:

1. Choice: Some level of control over how, what, and when students learn.
2. Competency: Adequate time, resources, and support to develop and master key skills.
3. Connection: Connecting learning to topics that actually matter to the learner.

When these three elements come together, transformative learning happens. We have seen it play out again and again in the lives of students who have broken free from traditional grading systems. Consider Olivia George, an OpenEd student who, at age 12, started a business called Mountain Blue Doodles. She wasn't just *studying* business, she was *living* it. When most kids her age were doing homework, she was working four jobs to save $2,100 for her first breeding dog. Marketing wasn't theoretical for her, it meant building a website that would convince skeptical adults to trust a teenage entrepreneur. When she faced challenges (and there were plenty), they weren't viewed as red marks on a report card, they were real problems that demanded real solutions.

"My parents loved me enough to allow me to fail," Olivia recalls. "They understood that success often comes after numerous failures, and instead of preventing me from experiencing disappointment, they let me learn from my mistakes."

The three Cs came together perfectly in Olivia's story. She had the freedom to choose her own path rather than follow a preset curriculum. She received the resources and mentorship needed to build real competency, from animal care to business management. And she was driven by a genuine connection to her work, breeding dogs that would change people's lives. The result was a thriving business that provides service and therapy dogs to families across the region, and more importantly, a young entrepreneur who mastered real skills by pursuing what mattered to her. You can't learn customer service from a worksheet, develop business acumen from a textbook, or build financial literacy through multiple choice tests. These skills come through the powerful combination of personal choice, supported learning, and genuine passion.

Choice is more than just picking your favorite flavor of ice cream. Real choice—the kind that drives deep learning—is about having agency over your educational journey. Research shows this kind of authentic choice leads to deeper engagement.[19] As psychology professor Dan Ariely has found, a person's willingness to work hard at something is directly tied to how meaningful they perceive the task to be.[20] Through freedom of choice, a young person who wants to learn something will often do it by whatever means are necessary. Providing various pathways to learning with supporting resources is much more valuable than forcing a singular set of tasks, assignments, or tests.

Competency means mastering skills at your own pace, with the support and resources needed. It is about demonstrating real capability, not just checking boxes.

Connection means linking learning to real life. Allowing children to explore their interests creates the authentic energy needed for them to learn to read, write, and do math. Learning, then, happens at the point where a child wants to not only learn something new, but also has recognized their own gap in knowing it. Real motivation to learn doesn't have to be forced.

> *Real motivation to learn doesn't have to be forced.*

Consider the Thygerson family, whose educational path led them from their local school in Utah to the foothills of Nepal. The Thygersons were just a regular family that decided to take education into their own hands in partnership with OpenEd. While their former classmates were memorizing facts for standardized tests, the Thygerson kids were designing safety vests, competing in robotics competitions, and yes, spending three months in Nepal, all on a modest budget. More importantly, they were learning how to learn. "The things that you learn when you travel are not in textbooks," one of the Thygerson children said of his education. "They're not just things that you're told. They're things that you experience and see firsthand." Each project became its own competency-based curriculum, where success meant actually creating something that worked or navigating the real world, not just scoring well on a test about how things work.

> *When students are allowed to focus on mastery rather than grades, they thrive.*

Across the country and around the world, schools and programs are proving that when students are allowed to focus on mastery rather than grades, they thrive. In Southern New Hampshire University's competency-based program, students demonstrate mastery through real-world projects rather than tests. In 2023, 70% of participating high school seniors graduated with college degrees before they even finished high school. Not because they were exceptionally gifted students, but because they were given the freedom to learn at their own pace and demonstrate mastery in their own way. Other universities across America have adopted competency-based education, as have entire countries like Finland and New Zealand. They have discovered that focusing on mastery rather than time spent in class better prepares students for a rapidly changing world.[21]

The model is surprisingly simple:

- Students progress at their own pace, with the freedom to pause when needed.
- Expectations are clear and transparent from the start.
- Multiple attempts are encouraged, converting "not yet" into mastery.
- Real-world application matters more than theoretical knowledge.

This philosophy can even be found in unexpected places. Look at the story of "Dumbledore's Army" in *Harry Potter and the Order of the Phoenix*. It's perhaps the greatest argument for competency-based learning in modern literature. When their traditional teacher refused to provide practical defense training, the students created their own learning environment. They practiced on their own time, focused on real-world applications, and supported each other's growth. Each student developed their strengths, motivated by a genuine need to learn. Although fictional, it's a perfect example of what education can look like when we trust learners to drive their own development.

The Freedom to Be Less Than Perfect

In a recent commencement address at Dartmouth, Roger Federer (the grade F tennis player, remember him?) reflected on his nearly 50% failure rate at the level of points played. "When you lose every second point on average," Federer explained, "you learn not to dwell on every shot. You teach yourself to think, 'Okay, I double faulted . . . it's only a point,' or 'Okay, I came to the net and got passed again . . . it's only a point.' Even a great shot, an overhead backhand smash that ends up on ESPN's Top 10 playlist, that too is just a point."[22]

Like planting a garden, improvement is like a steady drip line providing small amounts of water daily to nurture growth far better than flooding the entire area once a week, which drowns the seedlings. Learning works the same way. Small, daily progress, with plenty of room for mistakes, beats the high-pressure deluge of traditional education.

This mindset extends beyond sports. Consider Amy, Matt's wife and a mother of five who used to see those "World's Greatest Mom" mugs and feel like she could never measure up. Then she had an epiphany. What if being the World's Okayest Mom was actually enough? When her first grandchild was on the way, the family even printed her a World's Okayest Grammy t-shirt. It became their motto, right down to Amy's custom license plate: *OK EST.*

Isaac's grandfather, a rough-and-tumble, salt-of-the-earth WWII vet who loved working with his hands, used to say when he thought a project was done, "Good enough for who it's for." He was a prolific craftsman, churning out toys and bird feeders and kitchen utensils like a one-man factory. He wasn't trying to win any competitions, he was just trying to finish the task and enjoy the process. He never let perfection slow him down.

As Emily Stewart pointed out in a 2024 *Business Insider* article titled "The Joy of Average," our obsession with optimization and excellence in every area has backfired spectacularly.[23] We have created a world where being anything less than the best—whether as a parent, employee, or student—feels like failure. But what if, like Federer with his lost points, we learned to embrace the power of good enough in some areas so we can focus our energy where it matters most? That is the power of the "not yet" portion of the mastered or not yet model of learning.

Ask yourself this question, "Have you mastered everything there is to do on Earth?" Of course not. Even reading that probably made you laugh. Yes, we have mastered some things, but we are all a bunch of "not yets" at countless things, and that's okay; it's simply how life actually works. Think about instant replay in sports. When refs make a call on the field, they're making their best judgment with the information they have. But when new evidence comes in via replay, the fans don't consider it failure to change the call, we consider it progress. It's converting a "not yet" into a "mastered."

Every great chef has burned meals, every architect has crumpled up drawings (or deleted CAD files), and every scientist has run failed experiments. This is how we figure things out. No entrepreneur launches a perfect product on day one. No athlete performs flawlessly in their first game. Excellence comes through iteration, through the freedom to fail forward. But somewhere along the line, the established education system decided that each attempt was a final verdict. Get a C in algebra? That's it, you're a C student forever. Score poorly on a standardized test? Clearly, you're not a math person. Learning has morphed into a one-and-done performance instead of being viewed as a continuous journey of converting *not yets* into *mastered*.

> *Excellence comes through iteration, through the freedom to fail forward.*

Reimagine What's Possible

When 13 year old Logan LaPlante took the stage for his TED talk, "Hackschooling Makes Me Happy," he posed a question that stopped everyone in their tracks.[24] As he explained, adults were always asking him what he wanted to be when he grew up. They expected the usual answers such as astronaut, professional athlete, or neurosurgeon. But LaPlante had a different response: "When I grow up, I want to be happy."

Like computer hackers who modify systems to work better, LaPlante saw education as something to be reinvented, customized, and improved; hence, "hackschooling." A hacker mindset, he explained, means seeing a thousand possibilities where others see only one prescribed path. It sounds simple, maybe even naive. But LaPlante was tapping into something profound. While our education system rushes to prepare kids for careers, it often forgets to prepare them for life. He went on to identify eight key elements of a healthy, happy life, from exercise and nutrition to relationships and spirituality. He would continually ask traditional educators (and never got a satisfactory answer), "Why aren't these essential life skills considered as important as traditional academics?"

Rather than following any single curriculum or approach, hackschooling means taking advantage of community opportunities, learning through direct

> *When I grow up, I want to be happy.*

experience, and never losing sight of happiness and health as priorities. It's flexible, opportunistic, and focused on real-world application. Most importantly, LaPlante emphasized that any learner can adopt this mindset, not just homeschoolers. Whether you're in traditional school or learning independently, the key is to see education not as a rigid system but as something you can actively shape and improve.

There is an old Zen saying that illuminates why even wealthy people often wake up miserable. It states, "To be happy, one must strive to become a master of a challenging skill which one enjoys doing." Think about that for a minute. Kids who inherit fortunes or win the lottery often end up unhappy, despite their millions. Meanwhile, someone mastering a craft—whether woodworking or coding, teaching, or cooking—finds deep satisfaction even in the struggles. Finding a way to bless humankind with your skills adds even more depth to that satisfaction. When you connect personal mastery to making the world better, deep purpose emerges and genuine happiness expands.

Through hackschooling, LaPlante discovered the power of taking charge of his own education and finding the resources he needed to grow. This is what the Zen masters taught their students, and what more and more families are discovering. One of the most direct paths to happiness is learning something you're genuinely interested in, becoming really good at it, and finding a way to share it with others. The multiplier effect of this approach creates ripples of joy that extend far beyond the individual learner.

The pressure to conform to traditional education isn't just an American phenomenon. Consider the recent story of a family who fled China's educational pressure cooker for Thailand. In China, the drive for academic excellence has become so intense that parents literally upend their lives for it, quitting jobs and renting apartments near prestigious schools just to hover over their children's studies. They call it *peidu*, or "accompanied studying." But really, it's educational martyrdom. The Chinese have even coined terms for this exhausting race to nowhere. One is *neijuan*, the rat race that leads to burnout, and the other is *tang ping*, lying flat, or giving up entirely. It's telling that a culture had to invent multiple words just to describe educational burnout.[25]

Meanwhile in the UK, when officials proposed fining parents whose kids skip school, children's laureate Anne Fine pushed back with a radical suggestion: stop assuming every child is better off in traditional school. "Absenteeism," she argued, "should be thought of as, 'Here are a lot of children trying to tell us something. How can we accommodate what it is they're telling us?'"[26]

She's right. Today's record absenteeism isn't just about kids skipping school, it's about families voting with their feet. Before COVID-19, we might have dismissed alternative education as a fringe movement. Now we've seen that children can be self-aware, autonomous learners rather than empty vessels waiting to be filled.

The truth is, parents have far more flexibility than they realize. Most assume they are locked into rigid institutional schedules, but reality is more fluid. Consider the entrepreneur who loved having his daughter home during spring break so much that he dreaded sending her back to school. When told he could simply inform the school that she would be traveling with him for a few months, he was stunned. "Can I just do that? Won't the school be mad?" The school wasn't thrilled, but they couldn't stop him. His daughter had an incredible few months of learning through travel, returning to school when it made sense for their family. She wasn't dropping out, she was dropping in and out as needed. Once he realized this was possible, it transformed their approach to education. Like the family who left China's pressure cooker for Thailand, or the British parents pushing back against truancy fines, this father discovered that the traditional system's power exists largely in our minds.

Families everywhere are waking up to these possibilities. Education can be more flexible, more personalized, and yes, happier than we have been led to believe. The only question now is, "What's stopping you?"

With most parents feeling overwhelmed—almost half saying stress completely overwhelms them, according to a recent U.S. Surgeon General's report[27]—it's tempting to just default to the familiar, to let the system handle everything. After all, that's what schools are for, right? But what if that pressure comes from fighting against our instincts rather than following them? What if, like Federer focusing on the next point, families took it one step at a time? This isn't about throwing everything out overnight. This is about recognizing that education advances through people willing to try new approaches, to see the mountain of possibilities where others see only one prescribed path.

The question isn't whether your child should get an education, but whether they will get the education they actually need, one that develops not just their mind, but also expands their capacity for happiness and confidence, one that recognizes them as an individual with unique gifts to develop. The good news is you don't have to figure this all out at once. It starts with a shift in mindset.

In the next few chapters, we will explore what we call the open education mindset, a way of thinking about learning that can transform your family's educational journey, one small step at a time.

CHAPTER 3 RECAP:

- LeBron James would be considered a failure IF we were to grade him like we grade our kids.
- Standardized testing fundamentally misunderstands how humans learn, grow, and achieve mastery.
- A better way to think about learning is through competency-based education using a "mastered" or "not yet" approach.
- When students are allowed to focus on mastery rather than grades, they thrive.
- True learning happens at the intersection of three critical elements: choice, competency, and connection.
- We have created a world where being anything less than the best—whether as a parent, employee, or student—feels like failure. Let's embrace the "Joy of Average."
- "When I grow up, I want to be happy." LaPlante saw education as something to be reinvented, customized, and improved; hence, "hackschooling."
- The pressure to conform to traditional education isn't just an American phenomenon. Other countries face similar challenges.
- The truth is, parents have far more flexibility than they realize. Families everywhere are waking up to these possibilities. Education can be more flexible, more personalized, and yes, happier than we have been led to believe.

PART II

FIVE BUILDING BLOCKS FOR AN OPEN EDUCATION MINDSET

The winter of 1932 was particularly harsh in Billund, Denmark. Ole Kirk Christiansen stood in his empty carpentry workshop, surveying the remnants of what had once been a profitable business. The Great Depression had decimated his furniture orders, and his wife had recently passed away, leaving him with mounting debts and four sons between the ages of 6-15.

The Christiansen Solution

After reading an article in the magazine of the trade association to which he belonged, Christiansen was alerted to an opportunity to manufacture more readily marketable products like ladders, ironing boards, and wooden toys. It wasn't the path he'd imagined for himself. In better times, his workshop had produced fine furniture and architectural elements, pieces that required precision and skill. Now, he was crafting simple wooden cars and animals, selling them to local farmers who could barely afford necessities themselves. But amid this seeming setback, Christiansen noticed something remarkable. Children didn't just play with his toys as intended, they reimagined them. They took pieces apart and created new combinations he'd never envisioned. What looked like destruction to adult eyes was actually creative reconstruction through a child's imagination.

This observation eventually led to the creation of LEGO, a system where simple, interchangeable blocks could build almost anything. Christiansen's genius wasn't in creating complex, pre-built toys, but rather in providing fundamental building blocks that could be endlessly recombined.

You've seen the problems with the alternative, the one-size-fits-all approach to education, with its standardized tests, rigid schedules, and carbon-copy curriculum. You want something different for your children. But what? There are as many ways to learn as there are learners. Yet, just as simple LEGO bricks can create infinite possibilities, certain building blocks form the foundation of successful learning journeys. Throughout our combined 50+ years working with tens of thousands of families, we have seen these core elements combined and recombined in countless ways.

> *Just as simple LEGO bricks can create infinite possibilities, certain building blocks form the foundation of successful learning journeys.*

Unlike the linear conveyor belt of traditional schooling, these building blocks can be assembled in any order. You don't need every piece to begin building something beautiful. You might start with just one or two. You might emphasize different blocks at different times, experimenting with various combinations until you find what works. You can add pieces gradually. And most importantly, there is no single right way to put them together. The key is that even a few blocks, properly placed, create a foundation for whatever you want to build.

Parents who have unlocked an open education mindset have, in some form or another, adopted and adapted these five core building blocks:

- **Block #1: Embrace your child's uniqueness.** Like a gardener who understands that different plants thrive in different conditions, successful open educators celebrate what makes each child unique. This means resisting the urge to compare your child to others or measure them against arbitrary standards. When you stop asking "Why isn't my rose blooming as early as the neighbor's?" you can then focus more energy on creating a productive environment within your own garden.

- **Block #2: Put your kids before your reputation.** Pay attention to what is working for them without confusing it with the praise you get (or don't get) from others. Be secure in dispensing your duty as a parent—to help your child succeed—and don't conform to what gets the least criticism or makes you feel normal in the eyes of others. Parental social status seeking is one of the greatest obstacles to kids learning.

- **Block #3: Map the learning landscape.** Before any journey, you need to know your starting point and available resources. This often begins with a detox period, like clearing overgrown brush to see what naturally takes root. Then, through a series of explorations, you will map out three crucial territories: 1) your child's interests, 2) their needs, and 3) the resources at your disposal. This isn't a one-time survey, but an ongoing exploration you'll revisit throughout your journey.

- **Block #4: Give your child a voice.** Allow your child a majority vote in creating meaningful learning experiences. Start small and adapt along the way. Look for opportunities to apply the newly gained and interest-driven knowledge and skills to real-world scenarios. This partnership in learning builds not just knowledge but also agency and confidence. Your role shifts from director to co-explorer, guiding while remaining open to unexpected discoveries.

- **Block #5: Celebrate learner-driven sprints.** Just as nature moves in seasons, learning has its own rhythms. We call these "learning sprints," focused periods of exploration followed by celebration and reflection. These sprints build endurance and confidence over time. Each sprint adds to your child's portfolio of achievements, creating a tangible record of growth.

These blocks form the foundation of an open education mindset, but like any blueprint, they come alive through real application. While every family's journey is unique, seeing how others navigate this path can help you envision possibilities for your own. In the story that follows, we will watch one family discover and implement these building blocks in their own way. Though their specific situation may differ from yours, their struggles, discoveries, and triumphs echo those of thousands of families we've worked with over the years. Their story is fictional, but it's an amalgamation of real families, and their struggles and experiences are common.

Maya Learns Another Way

When Maya arrived at soccer practice—nearly 45 minutes after it started—her friend Olivia waved from the bleachers where she was watching their daughters practice. Like many parents, Maya was exhausting herself trying to make her family fit into an educational system that wasn't designed for them.

"Thanks for picking up Isabella," Maya said, dropping onto the bench beside her. "I don't know what I'd do without you these days."

"Of course," Olivia said. "We pass by her school anyway on the way to practice." She nodded toward the field where their daughters were running drills together. "Isabella's getting good with that left foot."

Maya tried to focus on the practice, but her mind kept drifting back to the afternoon's crisis. She pulled her jacket tighter against the autumn wind. "Had another thing with Kai today."

Anyone who has spent time around middle schoolers knows that the ages between 12 and 14 can be rough. But Kai's struggles went deeper. Now in 7th grade, he had been struggling since starting middle school, but this morning's homework meltdown had left Maya standing in his bedroom doorway, wondering which fire to put out first, her sobbing son or her daughter waiting at school.

"His teacher wants another meeting," Maya said. "She says his ADHD is getting worse, now that classes are harder." She watched Isabella execute a perfect pass. "At least he shows some emotion. Isabella used to love school, but lately . . ." She hesitated. "She spends hours building these incredible worlds in Minecraft. I mean, they're amazing, but her homework just sits there untouched."

"Sounds familiar," Olivia said quietly.

"And now Ava . . ." Maya shook her head. "You remember Ethan? My husband's brother in real estate?"

Olivia nodded.

"He's got Ava convinced she doesn't need college. She's ready to drop pre-med, and is talking about becoming an investor, starting her own business." Maya sighed, but managed a slight smile. "Marcus, my husband, hasn't said two words at dinner all week. His daughter, the future doctor, now wants to flip houses instead."

They watched in silence as the coach demonstrated a new drill. Isabella was paying attention now, focused in a way Maya rarely saw at home anymore.

"Three kids," Olivia said finally. "Three completely different paths."

"If only there was some standard solution that worked for all of them," Maya sighed. "Some magic formula."

Olivia turned toward her friend and smiled, a look of understanding and sympathy. "But that's exactly it, isn't it?" she said. "We keep trying to standardize something that can't be standardized. Your kids—all kids—are unique. What works for one . . ."

"Won't necessarily work for another," Maya finished. "I know you're right. I see it every day. But what am I supposed to do? Marcus and I both work full-time. I can't homeschool. And even if I could . . ." She lowered her voice, glancing around the crowded bleachers. "What would everyone think?"

Olivia smiled again, knowing exactly the struggle her friend was facing. She remembered having these same fears two years ago when Sophia was struggling. "Can I tell you about something that changed everything for our family? Remember when Sophia was in 4th grade?" Olivia asked, adjusting her scarf against the wind.

Maya thought back. Their daughters had been playing soccer together for three years now. "When she was having those anxiety attacks about tests?"

"That's right." Olivia watched her daughter demonstrating a move for Isabella. "Straight-A student when she was working at home with us. But put her in front of a test and she froze." She shook her head. "The school counselor wanted to put her in remedial classes. Said she needed extra support."

"But she's so bright," Maya said, watching Sophia explain something to Isabella. Both girls were laughing now.

"That's what kept me up at night," Olivia said. "I knew she understood everything. She just couldn't show it their way. You know what finally made me realize something had to change?

"What?"

"One morning I found her in the bathroom, pretending to be sick. Again. But this time she looked at me and said, 'Mom, I'm not really sick. I just can't do it anymore.' I was heartbroken because my little girl was struggling, and I didn't know how to help her."

Maya felt a familiar tightness in her chest. Just last week, she'd found Kai hiding in the basement before school.

"That's when I started looking into alternatives," Olivia continued. "Not to replace school entirely, just to open things up a bit. Give her some breathing room."

"What do you mean, 'open things up?'"

"Well, take Isabella's Minecraft worlds," Olivia said, "what if those became part of her learning instead of seeing it as an escape or a distraction and trying to compete with it?"

Maya turned to look at her friend. "How would that even work?"

"The same way we helped Sophia find her path. We started small, just one subject at a time. We found ways to connect what she loved doing with what she needed to learn." Olivia smiled. "You'd be amazed what kids can learn when they're building something they care about."

Maya watched Isabella sprint down the field. Her daughter was fully engaged now, calling for a pass, working with her teammates. She seemed so different from how she looked hunched over homework.

"But how do you actually do it?" Maya asked. "I mean, practically speaking. Marcus and I both work. I can barely keep up with their regular schoolwork as it is."

"That's what I thought too," Olivia said, "but here's what I didn't understand at first. We realized we were actually spending more time and energy fighting the *current system* than it would take to focus on supporting how our kids naturally learn."

The coach's whistle blew signaling to the girls to take a water break.

"Look at Kai," Olivia continued, "how much time do you spend trying to make him sit still and focus?"

"Hours," Maya admitted. "And then there's all the meetings, the calls from school, the . . ." She trailed off, counting the interruptions to her workday in her head. "My mother would love to help. She's offered to be with him during the day, but she's not a trained teacher. He's already behind in his grade and I don't want to add an extra problem by having him try to learn in an unstructured environment with my mom—sweet as she is—at the helm."

"And Ava?" Olivia asked gently. "How much time are you and Marcus spending trying to convince her to stick with pre-med?"

Maya sighed. "Marcus can barely look at her right now. He keeps saying it's too late to change direction. She's a junior, she's already on the college track."

"But she's passionate enough about real estate to take online courses on her own," Olivia pointed out. "When was the last time she showed that kind of initiative with her pre-med classes?"

Maya was quiet for a moment, watching Isabella jog back on the field, falling naturally into formation with her teammates. No one had to force her to learn soccer. She did drills willingly, practiced at home, and watched videos about technique. Because she wanted to.

"What if," Olivia suggested, "instead of fighting their interests, we worked with them? What if Ava's real estate became a way to learn economics, math, writing? What if Isabella's Minecraft games had actual learning goals built in? What if Kai could move around while he learns?"

Maya glanced upward, as if the answers would fall from heaven. "It sounds wonderful in theory," she said. "But I wouldn't even know where to start. And what would people think? The other parents, our families?"

Start small," Olivia said. "That's what we did. Want to grab coffee after practice? I can show you what those first steps looked like for us."

We see versions of Maya's story play out every week. Parents who realize that the standard education path isn't working for their family, and who feel trapped between their children's needs and the system's demands. A mother watching her ADHD son's spirit break a little more each day. Societal pressures masking a father's understanding that his daughter's entrepreneurial drive might be worth more than a specific degree or career path. A bright kid disappearing into mindless social media scrolling because school has become an exercise in compliance rather than curiosity.

The tipping point often comes in unexpected moments. For Maya, it was a soccer practice conversation that opened her eyes to possibilities she hadn't considered. For others, it's a child's tears over homework, or a teacher suggesting medication, or the quiet realization that the spark has gone out of their once-curious kid. What Maya, and thousands of parents like her, discover is that transforming their children's education isn't about following some prescribed alternative path. It's about having the courage to see what's already working—like Isabella's natural drive to create in Minecraft, or Ava's budding business sense—and building on those foundations.

Young people flourish when parents and educators embrace their natural inclinations rather than work against them. A 13-year-old who couldn't sit still in math class discovers geometry through building digital worlds. A high school junior who is falling behind in traditional classes shows sophisticated understanding of market analysis and deal structure through her real estate projects. What looks like distraction or rebellion in one context reveals itself as focus and initiative in another.

We are not suggesting that you let your kids do whatever they want. The families who succeed in opening up their children's education understand that structure matters, but it needs to be the right structure for each child. We have worked with thousands of families to develop customized approaches that maintain high standards while breaking free from standardization. If you are still looking to follow someone else's perfect formula, we have news for you. There isn't a perfect formula, and we believe that is cause for celebration. In fact, this philosophy is woven into the very identity of OpenEd.

( )penEd

Becoming an Open Education Designer

Look closely at our OpenEd company logo and you will notice something playful; it's an open parenthesis in place of the 'O.' It's not just clever design, it's an invitation to fill in your own approach. There are brackets or guardrails to provide some minimum level of safety and structure, but what goes in between them is wide open. We've learned that the most successful families aren't the ones who find the perfect system. Instead, they're the ones who feel empowered to become education designers and customize their children's learning journeys. Yes, choosing an open education path means making choices that might challenge conventional wisdom or raise eyebrows at family gatherings. But just as the LEGO toys' success proved Christiansen's insight correct—that creativity flourishes best within a framework of simple, flexible rules—we have seen thousands of families thrive when given the right building blocks for learning.

Every day at OpenEd, we work with parents who begin by saying, "I could never do that." They're looking for the perfect instruction manual, the guaranteed path to success. What they discover instead is something far more powerful. These forward-thinking parents become education designers. They begin to view a set of fundamental principles that, like LEGO bricks, can be combined in countless ways while still following clear guidelines. This is the true legacy of Christiansen's insight. He understood that innovation doesn't mean abandoning structure, it means creating the right kind of structure. LEGO bricks work because they follow precise rules of connection. Yet, within those rules, the possibilities are endless. Your child's education can work the same way.

In the next chapter, we'll explore what might be the most crucial building block of all. It's essential to view your child's unique traits not as problems to solve, but as foundations to build upon. In fact, through our work over the past few decades, we have discovered something counterintuitive. The very traits that often get labeled as problems in traditional schools—restlessness, obsessive interests, inability to sit still, dreaming, questioning—frequently become the cornerstones of a child's greatest achievements. The transformation can only happen if we see these characteristics differently, just as Christiansen saw possibility in what some dismissed as merely children breaking their toys.

CHAPTER 4 RECAP:

- OpenEd helps parents become "Open Education Designers" through these five core building blocks:
  - **Block #1:** Embrace your child's uniqueness.
  - **Block #2:** Put your kids before your reputation.
  - **Block #3:** Map the learning landscape.
  - **Block #4:** Give your child a voice.
  - **Block #5:** Celebrate learner-driven sprints.
- Like LEGO bricks, these principles can be combined in countless ways.

BUILDING BLOCK #1: EMBRACE YOUR CHILD'S UNIQUENESS

I n the 1950s, the U.S. Air Force had a problem. They had designed their cockpits based on the average measurements of hundreds of pilots from the 1920s. Yet these average cockpits seemed to fit no one well, leading to dangerous mistakes and near-misses. Something wasn't adding up.

What is Average?

Lieutenant Gilbert S. Daniels decided to measure over 4,000 pilots on ten critical dimensions. The question was simple, "How many pilots were average on all ten dimensions?" The answer was shocking. It turned out to be zero! Not a single pilot fit the average on all dimensions. The average pilot didn't exist. This discovery revolutionized aircraft design. Instead of building for the average, they started building adjustable seats and controls, which literally saved lives.

Designing for the average person means designing for no one. The Air Force learned this lesson decades ago, yet our education system is still stuck delivering pre-packaged, standardized education packages and wondering why they don't fit our children. After generations of designing education to fit every child and watching the unsatisfactory results, the traditional education system has yet to admit (or adjust to) the fact that every child develops in their own unique way, at their own pace.

Our understanding of the brain continues to deepen, revealing just how differently each one of us processes and learns. Research consistently shows that brain development begins before birth and continues throughout life, with each individual following their own timeline. After all, our bodies grow at different rates and we reach puberty and emotional maturity at different times as well. Child development experts at the Children's Hospital of Orange County (CHOC) confirm that children's growth patterns vary widely based on genetics, nutrition, physical activity, environment, and numerous other factors.[28]

The clearest evidence that standardization defies biology comes from studying twins. Even children sharing identical DNA and home environments develop at different rates. One twin might walk months before the other, just as one might master reading while the other excels at mathematics. Just how one may prefer bananas and the other applesauce, they also develop differently.[29]

In the early days of OpenEd, Matt and Amy Bowman surveyed 92 families with a simple question, "What is your favorite core curriculum for math, English, history, and science?" We expected clear winners in each category, something we could standardize around. Instead, we got 92 completely different responses. Even more surprising, we found different preferences within the same families. Perhaps no example illustrates this better than a conversation Matt had with a mother of triplet teenage girls. One might expect three children sharing identical DNA and environment would learn the same way. Yet, as she described their math education, her insight was remarkable. She pointed out that Jane and Jackie thrived with one type of curriculum while Julia needed something completely different. If even triplets required different approaches to learn effectively, how could anyone expect a standardized system to work for millions of unique children?

This was our true aha moment. That's when it clicked. True personalization in education means curating the best options and letting parents, teachers, mentors, and students choose what works best for them—by subject, grade, provider, and especially by child.

This biological diversity extends far beyond learning styles. Consider sleep patterns. Modern research on circadian rhythms shows that each person's natural sleep-wake cycle is unique. Yet, we force every teenager in a district to start school at the same early hour, regardless of their biological rhythms.

If even triplets required different approaches to learn effectively, how could anyone expect a standardized system to work for millions of unique children?

The Sleep Foundation's research confirms that most teenage brains are wired to fall asleep and wake later than adult brains.[30] When we ignore this biology, we create classrooms full of sleep-deprived learners, then wonder why they struggle to focus.

Our culture has recognized the need for personalization in most other areas of life. When we were growing up, the mentality was "You get what you get and don't throw a fit." Clothing came in basic sizes—S, M, L—and if it didn't fit, you made it work. Now, we rightly expect options for every body type. Food went through the same transformation. Once Burger King launched their "Have it Your Way" campaign, customization became the norm. Today, whether you are gluten-free, vegan, kosher, dairy-free, or have any other dietary need, restaurants and grocery stores accommodate your choice.

Our phones, our playlists, cars, entertainment, and nearly everything in modern life can be customized to individual preferences. Yet, somehow, we still expect children to learn the same material, at the same pace, in the same way, at the same time, in the same room. The next generation of learners—raised on personalization in every other aspect of their lives—increasingly reject this one-size-fits-all approach to education.

The Myth of the Average Student

Standardization becomes particularly problematic during adolescence, when development varies dramatically from child to child. During his years teaching middle school, Matt watched students transform at wildly different rates, not just physically but emotionally, socially, and intellectually.

The ages from ten to fourteen see more physical and psychological change than any other period except infancy. In a single 6th grade classroom, there might be one student who is 6'4" and another who is 4'6." Both developmentally normal. One might collect toy cars while another is already interested in driving them. One could need to shave daily while another shows no signs of facial hair. One might still play with dolls while another is going on dates. While one 14-year-old might experience their peak growth spurt, another in the same class might not start their major growth for another year or more. Yet, we expect these rapidly transforming young people to all learn the same material, at the same pace, in the same way. We group them strictly by birth year rather than developmental stage, creating situations where a physically mature 12-year-old might sit next to a peer who still looks and acts like a child.

This reality becomes even more striking at the edges of the bell curve. A landmark study launched at Johns Hopkins in the 1970s, "The Study of Mathematically Precocious Youth," has tracked thousands of students for over four decades. Its findings challenge our basic assumptions about learning. While the study focused on identifying and supporting gifted students, its most profound insight was broader. It concluded that when students are given opportunities to take courses aligned with their individual skills and interests—regardless of their IQ scores or grade levels—they consistently accomplish more than peers kept in standardized programs.

Consider Sam's story. In kindergarten, he was diagnosed as "profoundly gifted" only to be told by his public school principal,

"Your pace is too accelerated. The K–12 system has nothing more to offer you. Good luck on your own." Daunted, but not discouraged, Sam's mom began homeschooling him and found as many resources as she could to help him continuously learn and progress at his very accelerated pace. When Sam reached middle school, his mom discovered OpenEd and immediately enrolled him in the program. Eager to make the most of this opportunity, she attended several support meetings to learn more about how the program works and how to tailor it to Sam's unique needs. These meetings provided her with invaluable insights into the flexibility and resources available through OpenEd. Seeking advice from other parents in similar situations, Sam's mom joined the OpenEd Facebook group. There, she began asking questions about curricula and options other parents had found most effective for gifted children. The community's responses offered suggestions for advanced online courses, mentorship programs, and specialized curricula designed for gifted learners.

> *"Your pace is too accelerated. The K–12 system has nothing more to offer you. Good luck on your own." –An administrator to a gifted student*

Armed with this knowledge, Sam's mom curated an open education plan tailored to his needs that included accelerated math and science courses from top universities, advanced literature studies, and even online seminars with subject matter experts in fields that particularly interested Sam. She also incorporated hands-on projects and real-world applications of Sam's knowledge, ensuring his education remained engaging and challenging. Within a year, by age 13, Sam had completed several college-level courses with distinction. Sam's enrollment in the OpenEd public school program became a testament that the K–12 system still has much to offer students like Sam.

The need for flexibility extends far beyond academic giftedness. Another family shared how OpenEd adapted to their unique circumstances. "When the school year started," a parent shared with us, "my oldest was recovering from a serious injury and was uncomfortable with classmates seeing her feeding tube. OpenEd allowed her to continue her education while simultaneously recovering her health." Whether a child needs to move faster or needs space to heal, flexibility is the key. When children are allowed to learn in ways that suit them best, they don't just succeed academically, they discover their passions and develop a lifelong love for learning.

We have worked with thousands of students who were bored and wanted to go faster along their learning journey. They shouldn't be forced to hold back their curiosity and progress simply because others in their class learn at a different pace. Due to the constraints of traditional schooling, many teachers are forced to tell accelerated students who finish quickly to just read quietly until everyone else is finished. Or they tell more advanced students, "Go see if someone else needs help." Those default responses speak to the unfortunate reality that many teachers are ill-prepared and unsupported when they try to nurture and instruct students at different learning levels within the same classroom. And, for the most part, it isn't the teacher's fault. The nature of the system simply does not allow for that kind of flexibility.

We've also worked with struggling students who were left behind by their standardized schools. They needed help to regain confidence and address the gaps in their learning. These individual stories illustrate a broader truth that variation isn't the exception, it's the rule. As we saw with the mother of triplet girls, nowhere is this more evident than within families themselves.

When Matt and his wife, Amy raised their five children in the same nurturing home environment—with the same routines, rules, expectations, and opportunities—they noticed that each child developed in profoundly different ways. Despite identical parenting, each child showed unique interests, learning styles, and needs. This realization led Amy to make the observation that would shape their entire approach to education, as well as the original motto for OpenEd: "Our children are not standard."

Beyond personality differences, even their responses to the same educational environment varied dramatically. What worked beautifully for one child could be completely wrong for another, even among siblings experiencing the exact same school, teachers, and curriculum. One child might thrive in a traditional classroom while another needs to move to learn. One might accelerate through material while another needs more time to master concepts.

Every family with multiple children has observed the phenomenon that children from the same parents and raised in the same environment develop in remarkably different ways. It reflects a fundamental truth about human development that our standardized education system often ignores: there is no such thing as an average child.

> *"Our children are not standard."* — *Amy Bowman*

The Air Force's discovery about the myth of the average pilot was just one early example of a broader shift in how we think about human variety. The same insight that led to adjustable cockpits has emerged independently across industries. Today, streaming services create personalized viewing recommendations. Smartphones adapt their interfaces to individual usage patterns. Video games automatically adjust difficulty based on player performance. Industries across the board have embraced the reality that one size fits none. Everywhere except education, that is. It's a peculiar blind spot.

At education conferences, administrators nod vigorously when speakers talk about personalized learning. They share Sir Ken Robinson's viral TED talk about schools killing creativity. They quote extensively from research about different learning styles and brain development. The evidence that standardization fails our children is overwhelming and widely accepted. Yet, when Monday morning comes, these same educators return to schools designed around the myth of the average student. They continue the traditional grind, not because they don't care or don't understand. They do it because they are often afraid to do something different. The system itself—with its rigid schedules, standardized tests, and factory-model funding—is built to protect itself and dispel disruptors, which makes meaningful change seem impossible. Like pilots trying to fit into a cockpit designed for no one, educators and students alike contort themselves to fit a system that was never designed for human variety.

The good news is you don't have to wait for the entire system to change. While institutions struggle to adapt, individual families can take immediate action to customize their children's education. Today's world offers more resources, more flexibility, and more opportunities for personalized learning than ever before in human history. The journey begins with understanding your child's unique constellation of interests, needs, and available resources. But here's where many parents (ourselves included) hit our first real roadblock. Even when we see clearly what our child needs, we face an unexpected challenge that has nothing to do with curriculum, teaching methods, or learning styles. It's a challenge that shows up at family gatherings, manifests in sideways glances at the grocery store, and emerges in those seemingly innocent "How's school going?" conversations at neighborhood barbecues. It's the moment when what's best for your child conflicts with what others think is best for your reputation.

That challenge is one of the biggest stumbling blocks to adopting a liberated open education mindset. If you're going to overcome it, you'll need to tackle it head-on.

CHAPTER 5 RECAP:

- "Our children are not standard." —Amy Bowman
- Designing for the average person means designing for no one.
- Our phones, our playlists, cars, entertainment, and nearly everything in modern life can be customized to individual preferences. Yet, somehow, we still expect children to learn

the same material, at the same pace, in the same way, at the same time, in the same room.

- You don't have to wait for the entire system to change. While institutions struggle to adapt, individual families can take immediate action to customize their children's education. Today's world offers more resources, more flexibility, and more opportunities for personalized learning than ever before in human history.

CHAPTER 6:

BUILDING BLOCK #2: PUT YOUR KIDS BEFORE YOUR REPUTATION

The Powerful Force of Social Pressure

"I wish he was more like his sister." A mother told Isaac this while discussing her son joining the Praxis program instead of going to college.

The particular young man to whom she was referring was ambitious, sharp, and had lots of hustle and confidence. He had started a lawn care business and taught himself digital marketing. He was making upwards of $5,000 a month, enjoying life, growing, learning, and about to move into his own apartment. He was just 18. He had taken a semester of classes at community college before dropping out to focus on his business and self-taught marketing skills. He never liked school and got mediocre grades. He was excited about doing Praxis so he could get an apprenticeship at a tech startup and ramp up his marketing skills.

His mother was very concerned about him. She did not want him to drop out of community college. She did not want him to do Praxis. She wanted him to get a four-year degree. He caused her endless stress, which, apparently, his older sister did not.

Isaac asked, "What is his sister like?"

The mother's tone changed. Isaac could practically hear her glowing through the phone. She told him how her daughter had always been a great student. She got straight As through high school, took AP classes, got accepted to a good college, and graduated with honors.

He asked, "What's she doing now?"

The mother told him. She had been unable to get a job so far, nine months out of college. She'd moved back home, recently broken up with her boyfriend, and wasn't really sure what to do with her life. She was battling depression and trying to figure out how to pay off her student loan debt, as nobody seemed to be hiring in her area of study. She was applying to be a hostess at a local restaurant to get some cash while she decided what to do.

That was the moment Isaac realized the real hurdle to opening up the way we think about education, career, and success. It's not the inability to do things differently. It's not the lack of money or opportunity. Yes, those can be constraints, but they are usually easier to overcome than the biggest hurdle: parental pride.

This mother saw her depressed, indebted, dependent, aimless daughter as a flagship for family success. She saw her happy, money-making, independent, focused son as a cause for concern. This had nothing to do with how they were actually doing. It had everything to do with how other parents responded when she told them what her kid was up to. She was defining success for her kids by social status standards and the prestige of other parents, even while it was hurting her kids.

When someone asks at the barbeque, "How's Joey?" and you say, "In college," they will say, "Great!" and make you feel good. Even if Joey is unhappy, learning nothing, getting into debt, friendless, and getting drunk every night. College has become a proxy for success, so they just smile and assume he's good, which makes you feel like you've succeeded as a parent. If instead you say, "He's working and doing a few other things, trying to decide what's next," or worse, "He dropped out after a semester because he felt college wasn't the best option for him," you will immediately feel shame and embarrassment and notice concerned looks. Even if Joey is thriving.

Though most apparent with college, this social pressure and status-seeking applies across all levels of education. And it is a powerful force all parents must battle if we want what's best for our kids. It begins at birth. Well-meaning friends and family ask how much our kids weigh, whether they are walking, talking, learning to read, what grade they are in, etc. As parents, we feel immediate pressure to have normal answers to all of these questions. Social panic kicks in quickly, and we can sacrifice our kids on the altar of acceptance without even realizing it.

At the grocery store, a stranger smiles and says hi to your toddler who stares at them with a grumpy look. What's your instinct? Isaac admits that his instinct is to publicly chastise his kid and tell them to respond in kind. His immediate feeling is embarrassment that this stranger might think his kid is rude, and by extension, might think he's a bad parent. While there is value to raising polite kids who understand social conventions, we would argue that the better instinct is toward one's own kids. Why should we shame them for not greeting a total stranger? We owe nothing to this stranger besides basic civility, while our duties to our children are far graver, deeper, and more important.

This instinct to prove to others that your kid is okay and you're a good parent is pervasive. The grocery store greeting is a silly example with low stakes compared to education. But this same pressure can lead parents to make major decisions about their child's education based on social acceptance rather than on their children's needs.

Matt faced this pressure head-on when his 6th grade son came home one day and said, "My friend's mom mentioned a new charter school is opening next year. I really don't like my current district school. Can I go?" It was the first charter school in their area.

Having studied charter schools during his master's program, Matt was intrigued, but when he and Amy asked other parents how they felt about the new school, they were shocked by the extensive anger and animosity they encountered. The building wasn't even finished yet, and already the community was divided. Despite initial hesitation, they honored their son's wishes. It turned out to be exactly what he needed. He chose to stay through graduation, thriving in an environment that matched his learning style.

When their next two sons reached 7th grade (the charter school only served grades 7-12), both enrolled there too. One loved it and stayed through graduation. The other didn't like it and returned to his local school district after a year. Every decision was appropriate for that individual child, but the social pressure was intense. Matt, a former public school teacher himself, with Amy deeply involved as a school volunteer, faced strong pushback from their educator friends. They were accused of being "anti-district" (which they weren't) and abandoning the traditional path. Some claimed they were undermining community unity, though ironically, their neighborhood already had students attending multiple public schools through open choice options.

The pressure peaked when their second son (6'8" athletic) was at the charter school while his brother (6'6" equally athletic) attended the district school. Parents from the district school began lobbying hard. "You must act as the adult here and move him over," one dad insisted, convinced these tall brothers could secure a state basketball championship together. They simply couldn't understand how a parent could let a child decide where to go to school.

But Matt and Amy stood firm. Despite the guilt-slinging and the eyebrow-raising looks, they prioritized their children's happiness and wellbeing over community expectations. They stayed focused on helping their children lead their own education journeys, and have never regretted it. Each decision was valid because it served the individual child and resisted the social pressure to conform. How many kids fail to learn and thrive due to irrelevant standardized test scores, only because their parents are too scared to be judged by others if they get a bad grade or skip the tests altogether?

It is not easy to put your kids first. If you open up their education, you will face doubt and skepticism and subtle (and not-so-subtle) judgment from others. This will hurt, and it will make you doubt your path. In those moments, you have to bring your focus back to your kids. Keep asking yourself what helps them thrive. When you know one direction is better for them than the others, stick with it and stand firm against the social slings and arrows thrown at you. That's your job.

> *This instinct to prove to others that your kid is okay and you're a good parent is pervasive.*

As we mentioned earlier, standing for your kids and choosing an open education mindset can go both ways. Pulling your kid off the education conveyor belt into a more customized approach is hard. You may initially suffer for it. But if you persist, you will eventually find a tribe of like-minded parents and educators and it will feel less difficult. You may lose social status in the broader world, but you will eventually gain standing among other alternative educators, and the respect and appreciation of your kids. Then, a time may come when what's best for your kid is something a lot more similar to the standard school model. You might have to give up all your alt-ed cred with your new compatriots. That's okay.

Your role as a parent is to prepare your children to thrive as adults. You have to create the best environment for them, which often means protecting them from the (often well-intentioned) expectations and norms of others, rather than adding to the confusion with your own wishes for their future. This doesn't mean having no standards or expectations for your kids. Part of parenting is pushing them to be their best and encouraging them to take on challenges. It does mean ensuring that any expectations you put on them are what you know they need, not what the world assumes they need. Parenting is a series of small steps where you prioritize your children over yourself. Time and resources are known and accepted sacrifices for most parents. But if you don't also let go of your need to be admired, praised, or approved of by other adults, you could put all your time and money into something that makes your kids miserable. We can't stress this enough. This is about your kids, not your reputation.

CHAPTER 6 RECAP:

- The social pressure and status-seeking is a powerful force all parents must battle if we want what's best for our kids.
- This instinct to prove to others that your kid is okay and you're a good parent is pervasive.
- Pulling your kid off the education conveyor belt into a more customized approach is hard.
- Parenting is a series of small steps where you prioritize your children over yourself.
- We can't stress this enough. This is about your kids, not your reputation.

BUILDING BLOCK #3:
MAP THE LEARNING LANDSCAPE

Three Elements of Learning

In 2012, a one-ton robotic explorer named Curiosity touched down on Mars. Its mission was to search for signs of ancient microbial life, study the Martian climate and geology, and assess whether the Red Planet could have ever supported life. But long before Curiosity began its journey, NASA's engineers faced a more immediate challenge. They were tasked with designing something to explore a world no one has ever visited. They couldn't rely on previous blueprints or standard designs. Mars, with its harsh dust storms, extreme temperature swings, and unique geological features, demanded fresh thinking.

The team started by asking three fundamental questions that would shape every aspect of the mission:

1. What does Mars need us to discover? (The mission objectives.)
2. What unique capabilities can we develop? (Their areas of innovation.)
3. What resources do we have? (The technical and material constraints.)

This systematic approach to exploring uncharted territory offers a surprising parallel for parents navigating their children's education. Like Mars, each child's mind is a unique landscape waiting to be explored. And like NASA's engineers, parents need to understand three key elements of learning before beginning their journey:

1. What naturally drives your child's curiosity? (Interests)
2. What does your child's environment require? (Needs)
3. What tools and opportunities are available? (Resources)

When these elements align—like the perfectly calibrated instruments on Curiosity—learning becomes a journey of discovery. Every child's learning journey of curiosity is shaped by their experiences, surroundings, and natural interests. Their curiosity is fed by the needs of family, home, neighborhood, and community. The resources available to support their learning vary widely, but they all combine to influence and guide their path forward. Just as NASA's engineers had to work within the constraints of physics, budget, and available technology while still pushing the boundaries of what's possible, parents need to understand our constraints while remaining open to creative solutions.

Connecting Interests, Needs, and Resources to Learning

Consider a time in your life when you were excited to learn something. Maybe it was mastering an instrument during elementary school, learning a family recipe during summers with grandparents, or diving into a complex project on your first day at a job. Think back to that feeling of genuine enthusiasm, the way time seemed to stop when you were engaged in deep learning. Now, remember who else was learning alongside you. Perhaps there were classmates, siblings, or coworkers sharing the same experience. Yet, despite being exposed to the same material, each person gravitated toward different aspects of what was being learned. One musician might have been fascinated by theory while another lived for performance. One cook might have focused on perfecting traditional techniques while another experimented with creative variations.

This natural diversity of interests is a feature, not a bug, of human learning. Just as we wouldn't expect every engineer at NASA to be equally passionate about propulsion systems versus atmospheric analysis, we can't expect every child to engage with subjects in the same way. One 10-year-old might lose themselves for hours in mathematical puzzles while another comes alive during creative writing. A third might struggle with both but show remarkable intuition for scientific experiments and collaboration.

The power of open education lies in recognizing and working *with* these natural variations rather than *against* them. But interest alone isn't enough. Think back to your own learning experience again. As you developed that new skill or knowledge, you likely found yourself considering how it could be useful to yourself on a broader scale, to your family or your community. The more you could see its potential value, the more motivated you became to master it. This leads to the second element of the learning journey, which is needs. When we connect a child's natural interests to real needs in their world, learning takes on new meaning and purpose.

Finally, remember the resources that supported your learning journey. Maybe it was a patient mentor, a well-equipped workspace, or simply having enough time to practice. You probably found yourself seeking additional resources as your interest grew, perhaps borrowing books from the library, watching instructional videos, or connecting with others who shared your passion. The third crucial element of the learning journey is having access to the right resources, tools, and support at the right time.

By aligning these three elements—**interests**, **needs**, and **resources**—a child's learning journey ignites. Their interests lead them towards engaging in real-world challenges. This can then actually help them discover what they *don't* enjoy, an important

> *By aligning these three elements — interests, needs, and resources — a child's learning journey ignites.*

step toward finding what they do like. This work provides context and purpose to their learning. Now, the resources at their disposal become tools, not just for personal growth, but also for making a tangible difference in their world.

The process begins with three fundamental steps that form the foundation of your child's open education pathway.

Step 1: Discover Interests

Step 2: Identify Needs

Step 3: Analyze Available Resources

These steps will help you identify and nurture your child's interests while building the skills of deep learning, of learning how to learn.

Step 1: Discover Interests

After your child has had time to detox and decompress, they will be ready to enter a new phase of learning. This exercise helps them identify their interests.

First, create a Discovery Zone in your home—a wall, poster board, or whiteboard where family members can post sticky notes. Place stacks of notes in easily accessible spots around the house. Over the course of a week, invite everyone in the family to ponder and post answers to five key questions:

1. What do I like to learn about?
2. What do I like to do or think about in my free time?
3. What do I believe I'm good at doing?
4. What am I not yet good at, but would like to improve?
5. What activities do I genuinely dislike and have no interest in developing?

The responses might surprise you. They often range from dinosaurs and space to sports and animals, from music and dance to robots and coding, from rocks and plants to movies and puzzles. Each note represents a potential path for exploration.

Often, the tension between ambitious ideas and real-world constraints is where the most meaningful learning occurs.

For this exercise to work best, the entire family must commit to making it a judgment-free zone. Celebrate wild and unrealistic ideas instead of criticizing them. Encourage open thinking and big dreams. It's easy to predict setbacks ahead, but don't do it. Often, the tension between ambitious ideas and real-world constraints is where the most meaningful learning occurs.

After a week, gather as a family to discuss what you've discovered. Use the "Discover Your Interests" tool shown below to organize these thoughts and look for patterns. Pay special attention to overlapping interests—these can suggest activities for the whole family. These notes will guide your next steps, so keep them handy. These tools and other resources are available at opened.co/book.

DISCOVER YOUR INTERESTS

What I Like to Learn About:

_____

_____

_____

What I Do in My Free Time:

_____

_____

_____

What I'm Good At:

_____

_____

_____

What I Want to Improve:

_____

_____

_____

What I Don't Enjoy:

_____

_____

_____

Common Themes I Notice:

_____

_____

_____

Step 2: Identify Needs

"Why do I need to learn this?" is a question every parent has heard, and it deserves a better answer than "Because it's on the test." Real learning happens when children see how their interests connect to actual needs, in their lives, their families, and their communities. Learning sticks when it solves real problems. When children can apply their knowledge and skills to tangible challenges, their motivation soars. This isn't just true for kids; people of all ages learn best when they can see the direct impact of their efforts. Use the "Identify Your Needs" tool shown below to help you map these connections, starting with your immediate family's needs.

Take time to consider your household's day-to-day needs, everything from managing sleep schedules and preparing meals to balancing work time and maintaining relationships. Think about household responsibilities, financial planning, quality time for conversations, screen time limits, hobbies, travel, and preparation for the future. This inventory will help ensure your child's learning plan aligns with your family's real requirements.

Next, broaden your view to identify challenges in your wider community. For older children, this might include exploring significant societal issues like hunger, poverty, homelessness, environmental concerns, or public health. But don't feel pressured to tackle only big problems. For younger children especially, focus on tangible challenges they can observe and potentially help address, such as trash in the local park, a vacant lot needing care, lonely neighbors, worn-down fences, broken playground equipment, or classmates lacking basic supplies. If you need inspiration, visit JustServe (https://www.justserve.org/) and search for service projects in your town to get a sense of what your community needs.

Finally, organize these challenges by scope, creating a map from personal to global: self, home and family, neighborhood and community, state, country, and world. This framework helps children see how their actions can create ripples of change, starting with their immediate environment and potentially extending much further.

Take a week to complete this exercise, discussing the possibilities as a family. Again, keep these notes handy. You will be surprised how often opportunities arise to connect your child's interests with real needs in your home or community.

IDENTIFYING YOUR NEEDS

Instructions: Use this tool to identify needs at different levels, from your immediate family to broader community issues. For each line, write specific needs, challenges, or opportunities you observe. Examples are provided in parentheses to help guide your thinking.

Family Needs

- Daily Routines: _____
  (e.g., after-school supervision, coordinated meals, morning schedules)
- Workspace: _____
  (e.g., homework areas, project spaces, quiet study zones)
- Family Activities: _____
  (e.g., shared meals, game nights, outdoor time)
- Project Management: _____
  (e.g., supply tracking, schedule coordination, documentation)

Community Challenges

- Local Support Needs: _____
  (e.g., senior assistance, tutoring programs, neighborhood initiatives)
- Educational Gaps: _____
  (e.g., STEM programs, arts education, special needs support)
- Environmental Issues: _____
  (e.g., park maintenance, recycling programs, community gardens)
- Youth Programs: _____
  (e.g., after-school clubs, sports teams, mentorship opportunities)

Broader Issues

- Environmental: _____
  (e.g., conservation projects, sustainability initiatives, local cleanup)
- Education: _____ (e.g., access to resources, specialized programs, technology gaps)
- Community Development: _____
  (e.g., public spaces, shared resources, local improvement projects)
- Digital Access: _____
  (e.g., technology training, internet access, device availability)

Opportunities for Impact

Connecting the interests and skills with an identified need can create an impact. For example: "Coding skills + struggling students = organize an after-school tutoring program."

- Skill + Need = Impact: _____
- Skill + Need = Impact: _____
- Skill + Need = Impact: _____
- Skill + Need = Impact: _____

Next Steps: Review your entries and identify two to three immediate opportunities where your family's interests and skill development are aligned with specific community needs.

Step 3. Analyze Available Resources

After identifying your child's interests and connecting them to real needs, it's time to survey the tools and resources available to you. True learning happens inside *learners*, not *buildings*. Keep in mind that your available resources extend far beyond the walls of your home and school. Use the "Analyzing Your Resources" tool shown below to help you get started.

Before diving into specific resources, take a moment to consider what are the main *"jobs to be done"* that you're *"hiring"* the school or program to do your family. This is a concept Professor Clayton Christensen developed to help identify why customers choose specific products or services.[31] When parents evaluate why they want to "hire" a particular school or program, they will likely look for things such as:

- Safe childcare during work hours
- Social interaction with peers
- Academic preparation for college
- Development of specific skills
- Character development and mentorship

Discuss how you would rank the order of importance of these five attributes based on what you would want a school or education program to provide for your family.

Next, use the sample resources listed in this chart and begin to evaluate the affordability of each one. We've organized the chart into three columns ranging from free/low cost to higher cost.

Free/Low Cost	Moderate Investment	Special Opportunities
Public library (books, audiobooks, workshops)	Museum memberships	Professional certifications
Khan Academy and Code.org	Community education classes	Early college programs
Community centers and parks	Sports leagues and clubs	Apprenticeships
Family expertise and connections	Online courses (Outschool, Coursera)	Specialized camps
Educational YouTube channels	Local tutoring exchanges	Private instruction
Public school à la carte options	Homeschool co-ops	Microschools

ANALYZING YOUR RESOURCES

Important "jobs to be done"

Which of these "jobs to be done" by a school or program are the most important to you? Rank the five items on this list in order of importance from 1-5:

- Academic Development   _____
- Social Interaction   _____
- Skill Building   _____
- Character Development   _____
- College/Career Preparation _____

Available resources we already have:

(i.e. access to physical spaces/classrooms, libraries, labs, gyms, community centers, teachers, mentors, classes, curriculum, materials, services, tools, software, hardware, etc.)

Resources we need to get:

(i.e. access to physical spaces / classrooms, libraries, labs, gyms, community centers, teachers, mentors, classes, curriculum, materials, services, tools, software, hardware, etc.)

Action items this week:

1. Research _____ Who will do it? _____
2. Call _____ Who will do it? _____
3. Purchase _____ Who will do it? _____

The objective isn't to find every possible resource. The point is to identify the right resources for your child's interests and needs. Start small, focusing on readily available options that align with the interests and needs you identified in Steps 1 and Step 2. You might be surprised how many resources are already within reach.

Now, let's check in and see how Maya and her family connected their interests, needs, and resources to learning.

Maya's Discoveries

Three weeks had passed since that pivotal conversation at soccer practice. Maya and Olivia's quick chat over coffee had turned into a two-hour strategy session, with Olivia sharing templates and exercises she'd developed during her own family's transition. Maya had left with a stack of sticky notes and a mix of hope and skepticism.

Now, gathered around their dining room table on a Sunday evening, the evidence of those three weeks covered nearly an entire wall. Yellow notes captured Ava's growing interest in real estate and business. Pink ones revealed Isabella's fascination with chemistry and experiments. Blue notes showed Kai's varied interests, scattered but showing clear patterns for his family who had learned to look beneath the surface. Even Marcus—the buttoned-down medical professor—initially reluctant to this process, had added his own observations on green notes. What had started as a simple exercise had become a family ritual. Each evening, someone would quietly add another note to the wall. Sometimes they would catch each other reading them, sparking unexpected conversations. The wall had become a map of possibilities, each note a potential pathway to explore.

The wall had become organized around five key questions, with each family member's responses on different colored notes:

Ava (yellow notes):

What do you like to learn about?
- *How real estate deals actually work*
- *Uncle Ethan's investment strategies*

What do you think about in your free time?
- *Ways to find undervalued houses*
- *Starting a student investment club*

What are you good at?
- *Making spreadsheets make sense*
- *Explaining business stuff to others*

What do you want to improve?
- *Understanding mortgages*
- *Public speaking for presentations*

What do you not enjoy/don't want to develop?
- *Memorizing biology terms*
- *Lab reports and clinical studies*

Isabella (pink notes):

What do you like to learn about?
- *Why things react together*
- *Stories about women scientists*

What do you think about in your free time?
- *New experiments to try*
- *What happens if you mix stuff together*

What are you good at?

- *Measuring ingredients / taking steps precisely*
- *Following scientific method*

What do you want to improve?

- *Real lab techniques*
- *Using proper equipment effectively*

What do you not enjoy/don't want to develop?

- *Writing detailed lab reports*
- *Regular cooking (it's too simple!)*

Kai (blue notes)

What do you like to learn about?

- *How to teach Minecraft to others better*
- *Good ways to explain hard stuff*

What do you think about in your free time?

- *Making tutorial videos*
- *Helping other kids learn*

What are you good at?

- *Helping frustrated kids*
- *Breaking down complex things*

What do you want to improve?

- *Making clearer videos*
- *Skills for teaching bigger groups*

What do you not enjoy/don't want to develop?

- *Sitting still in class*
- *Working by myself*

Maya studied the wall of notes while Marcus cleared the dinner dishes. She noticed patterns she hadn't seen before. Kai's notes, though fewer in number, showed a clear theme including, "I like helping younger kids with math," "Good at explaining games," "Want to teach others Minecraft." His struggles with traditional learning hadn't dampened his natural inclination to teach.

"Come look at this," she called to Marcus.

He dried his hands and joined her at the wall. "Interesting timing," he said. "Mrs. Chen asked today if Kai could help with the after-school coding club. Said he has a way with the frustrated kids."

Their conversation was interrupted by the sound of mixing bowls clanking in the kitchen. Isabella had already started her evening ritual, what she called her "kitchen chemistry." Since Maya's suggestion about baking, the experiments had grown more ambitious.

"Mom!" Isabella's voice carried from the kitchen. "How much does baking soda react with vinegar?"

Maya glanced at Marcus and smiled, then pulled her planning sheets from under the stack of notebooks. Her lists and annotations from their first meeting with Olivia had evolved into something more structured. Looking at it now, next to the wall of interests, she felt a flutter of pride. Their messy brainstorming was transforming into real plans.

MAYA'S IDENTIFIED NEEDS

Family Needs:

- Daily Routines: After-school coverage, coordinated meals, everyone's schedules, clean rooms, dishes, laundry, food, etc.
- Workspace: Project areas, homework space, experiment zones
- Family Activities: Game nights, shared meals, weekend planning
- Project Management: Supply tracking, documentation, schedules

Community Challenges:

- Local Support: Senior tech help, tutoring programs
- Educational Gaps: STEM opportunities, library volunteers
- Environmental Issues: Park projects, creek cleanup
- Youth Programs: After-school clubs, mentorship

Broader Issues:

- Environmental: Watershed programs, recycling initiatives
- Education: Access to programs, specialized learning
- Community Development: Public spaces, shared resources
- Digital Access: Training programs, technology gaps

Potential Connections:

- Kai's teaching + kids struggling with tech = After-school coding club
- Isabella's experiments + science education = Community lab program
- Ava's business skills + local needs = Youth entrepreneurship club
- Family expertise + neighborhood needs = Skills sharing network

The front door opened and Ava walked in, carrying a stack of library books. "I found these for you, Bella," she said, setting them down. "Basic chemistry, lab safety, and . . ." she pulled out the last book with a flourish, "the history of women in science."

"Did you get the one about Marie Curie?" Isabella asked.

"Better. Got one written by her daughter."

Maya watched her daughters huddle over the books, their heads together, pointing at diagrams. Three weeks ago, they'd barely spoken to each other. Now Ava's business planning skills were helping shape Isabella's scientific ambitions.

While Isabella and Ava explored their books, Kai appeared in the doorway, lingering as he often did when unsure whether to join in. But tonight was different. He held his own notebook.

"I made a list too," he said quietly. The pages were filled with his distinctive mix of words and drawings, a mind map of everything he wanted to learn about teaching younger kids.

"Show them the schedule part," Ava said, not looking up from the chemistry book.

Kai flipped to the back page. He had outlined a plan to split his time between regular classes and helping with the coding club. Mrs. Chen had already approved it, pending their parents' permission.

"And look what I found," he said, pulling out his phone. The screen showed a free course on peer tutoring basics. "The librarian helped me find it. She said I could use the study room to take it."

Maya felt Marcus shift beside her. They had spent years trying to get Kai to sit still for lessons. Now, here he was, independently finding resources for something he cared about.

"There's more," Kai said. He hesitated, then continued. "Grandma said she could drive me to the elementary school three days a week. She wants to volunteer there too."

The kitchen had grown quiet. Even Isabella had stopped measuring. They all knew what this meant. This would be their first real test of flexible scheduling.

"Show them the outcomes page," Ava prompted. Always the business mentor, she'd helped Kai create clear goals and measurements.

"It's not finished," he mumbled.

"Show them anyway," his sister urged.

Kai's outcome page was simple but powerful. Three columns: What I'll Learn, Who I'll Help, How We'll Know It's Working. The last column included both academic metrics and personal goals. "Feel confident teaching others" was at the top of his list.

Maya felt a deep sense of joy. Seeing the progress her children were making helped her know all of the hard work was worth it. Here's a copy of the plans:

Available resources we already have:

- Physical Spaces: Kitchen for experiments, Uncle Ethan's shed for real estate discussions, video corner for Kai, local library
- Available Support: Grandma's help (T/W/Th), Marcus's medical contacts
- Current Tools: Basic lab supplies, video equipment, library cards
- Programs: Mrs. Chen's coding club at the library
- Learning Materials: Ava's business books, Isabella's science equipment

Resources we need to get:

- Dedicated project area, tutoring space, Lab safety equipment
- Stronger internet connection
- Transportation plan, liability insurance
- Science mentor for Isabella, real estate courses for Ava
- Advanced lab equipment, professional video setup, software licenses

Action items this week:

1. Research: video software options   Who will do it? Kai
2. Call: local real estate trainer   Who will do it? Ava
3. Purchase: Lab safety equipment   Who will do it? Isabella

"Mom?" Isabella glanced over her shoulder. "We should add a microscope to that list."

Marcus laughed. "One step at a time. We've got quite a few items to figure out first."

"Speaking of which . . ." Maya pulled out Kai's proposal from under the stack. His plans for the coding club had seemed ambitious this morning. But now, looking at their growing list of resources and Isabella's careful planning, it felt less daunting.

Before she could say more, Isabella's voice cut through her thoughts. "If I can have a lab," she said, still focused on her measurements, "Kai should be able to have a classroom."

Later that night, after the kids had gone to bed, Maya and Marcus sat at their kitchen table reviewing the wall of notes, the lists, and the plans their children had created. The same table where, three weeks ago, they'd hesitated to even start this journey.

"Remember what Olivia said?" Maya asked, sorting through Isabella's notebook. "About how it starts with small changes?"

Marcus nodded, still studying Kai's outcome page. "Small changes adding up to something bigger."

The evidence was there on their wall; a map of possibilities that hadn't existed a month ago. Isabella's scientific interests connecting to real-world skills. Kai's struggles transforming into strengths. Ava mentoring her siblings while pursuing her own path. Even their extended family was being drawn into this web of learning and support.

This wasn't the dramatic transformation they'd initially feared would be necessary. Instead, it was a series of small, intentional steps, including putting up sticky notes, identifying needs, and finding resources that were often already available. Each step revealed new possibilities, each small success built confidence for the next change.

Before heading to bed, Maya added one final sticky note to the wall: "Trust the process."

Remember that you don't need to revolutionize everything at once. Start with one interested child, one identified need, one available resource. Let small changes add up to meaningful transformation. The journey to open education isn't about sudden upheaval, it's about intentional exploration, one step at a time.

In the next chapter, we'll explore how to give your child a voice in this process, turning these discoveries into actionable learning plans.

CHAPTER 7 RECAP:

- By aligning these three elements—interests, needs, and resources—a child's learning journey ignites.
- Discover Interests:
  - ○ Choose your documentation method (wall, notebook, digital).
  - ○ Have each family member answer the five key questions.
  - ○ Set aside time to discuss patterns and connections.
  - ○ Look for overlapping interests and opportunities.
- Identify Needs:
  - ○ Start with daily family requirements.
  - ○ Look for community challenges you can address.
  - ○ Consider broader impact opportunities.
  - ○ Connect interests and skills to specific problems.
- Analyze Available Resources:
  - ○ Rank the "jobs to be done" by your school or program.
  - ○ List the available resources you already have.
  - ○ Identify the resources you need to get.
  - ○ Assign specific action items for this week.

CHAPTER 8:
BUILDING BLOCK #4: GIVE YOUR CHILD A VOICE

Minecraft as Education?

Markus Persson spent his childhood taking things apart. While other kids played with toys as intended, he disassembled them to understand how they worked. At nine, he dismantled his father's Commodore 128 computer. When he couldn't figure out how to put it back together, he taught himself programming instead. This same spirit would later lead him to create Minecraft, the second best-selling game of all time (second only to Tetris).[32]

Persson's creation broke every rule of game design. There were no instructions, no levels, and not even any clear objectives. There were just digital blocks and infinite possibilities. Parents worried their kids were wasting time. Teachers banned it from schools. Yet, within a decade, the Minecraft franchise would become not just a global phenomenon, but a revolutionary educational tool used in over 115 countries. Why? Because Persson understood something fundamental about human nature. He knew that when young people have true agency, deep learning happens. The success of Minecraft in education was, by traditional standards, impossible.

> *Children who guide their own education develop stronger critical thinking skills, greater intrinsic motivation, and perhaps most importantly, a deeper love for learning.*

Naomi Clark, chair of the NYU Game Center shares, "What Minecraft Education offers is a path toward high-quality, concentrated screen time that aligns with a curriculum, while maintaining the open-ended nature of a game where players can sort of decide to do what they're interested in and pursue their goals." In other words, it succeeds precisely because it breaks the rules traditionalists thought were essential for learning.

Max Brooks, author of a popular trilogy of Minecraft books, puts it more bluntly. He said, "Minecraft has the potential to be the greatest educational tool since Gutenberg's printing press." Why? Because it fundamentally challenges how we think about learning. "The education system that you and I had," Brooks explains, "is the Prussian model of education—standardization, rote memorization, regurgitation, under a ticking clock. That was the perfect education model for the industrial revolution. But that doesn't work anymore."

So, what does work? As we saw earlier in this book, Ole Kirk Christiansen discovered the same essential truth as the Minecraft creator did decades earlier in his workshop in Billund, Denmark. What began as simple wooden toys evolved into something revolutionary, a system where basic pieces could create anything their creator could imagine. The LEGO system, like Minecraft after it, wasn't about prescribing what children should build, it was about providing the fundamental building blocks and letting their creativity soar. This combination—clear structure with boundless possibilities for creativity—isn't just clever game design or toy making; it's a blueprint for how children naturally learn.

So, how do we put this into practice? The journey begins with something many parents find counterintuitive: stepping back and allowing time for curiosity to naturally rekindle.

Rekindle Your Child's Curiosity

Building an open education mindset takes time. Don't expect an overnight transformation. The first step, which many parents find challenging, is creating space for your child's natural curiosity to re-emerge. As Zig Ziglar reminds us, "You don't have to be great to start, but you have to start to be great."

Most young people beginning the journey to become a self-directed learner need a little time to detox from the traditional schooled mindset. Even if you do not plan to remove your kids from school, you can and must work to remove the schooled mindset from your routines and habits. This detox period may take anywhere from two days to two weeks or more. Be patient. The older a child is, the longer it may take to unleash their natural creativity and curiosity, which is why starting young can be helpful. This insight isn't limited to children. Several of our adult children have shared that they still need regular reminders to step back from their daily grind and reconnect with their love of learning. The patterns we develop early tend to stay with us.

When you begin this journey with your family, start by sharing your vision for exploring a new direction together. Open with simple questions such as, "If we could design your education from scratch, where would you want to start? What if you had more freedom to explore what interests you?" Be prepared for a range of reactions, from excitement to uncertainty. Some children might immediately ask, "Does this mean no more school?" or they might worry, "Will I still see my friends?" Reassure them that this is about *opening* doors, not *closing* them. Ask what they have always wanted to learn more about, or which parts of school they've most enjoyed. This conversation begins their journey toward taking ownership of their education.

Next, comes what we call the "unwind phase." This is where many parents struggle. Your instinct might be to immediately structure this time to ensure it's productive. Resist this urge. Real transformation requires genuine rest. Let your child catch up on sleep. Traditional school schedules often create chronic exhaustion. Allow them to decompress through unstructured play, video games, or movies for a bit. Make interesting books available without pressure to read them. Their brain needs this fallow period to prepare for self-directed learning. Watch for signs that your child's natural curiosity is reawakening. You might notice them asking more questions, showing interest in new topics, or spending longer periods focused on activities they choose. When you see these sparks of genuine interest—not when you think enough time has passed—you can begin exploring more structured activities together.

If your child expresses interest in a specific project, by all means support them. But be careful not to replace one rigid structure with another. Here are a few examples of how children of different ages might naturally begin engaging:

- A young child might spend hours building increasingly complex LEGO structures, naturally developing spatial reasoning and problem-solving skills.
- A middle schooler could become fascinated with cooking, learning fractions and chemistry through experimentation in the kitchen.
- A teenager might dive into Minecraft architecture, creating detailed replicas of historical buildings that combine creativity with research skills.

The key here is to follow their lead rather than imposing projects. Some children might want to organize the garage or plant a garden. Others might prefer documenting family recipes or learning small engine repair. Oftentimes, your own enthusiasm for a project might be contagious ("Who wants to help me sort these old family photos into an album?"). The specific activity matters less than the fact that it emerges from genuine interest.

Remember to resist the common parental urge to over-structure this phase. The goal is to help their brain reset from the daily grind of standardized schooling and gain a sense of independence in the process. Even when it seems like they're not doing anything productive, your child is learning something invaluable. Help them learn how to be comfortable with unstructured time and how to follow their curiosity. This skill will serve them far better than any specific project you might design.

Trust Them to Find Their Own Way

Matt learned one of his most valuable parenting lessons not at home, but on a soccer field. After years of coaching his own kids in various sports, he found himself as an assistant coach to a friend who had an unusual approach to building his team. This friend had studied and coached athletes at all different levels, and his unique insights left a lasting impression on Matt. Though cancer took his friend's life several years ago, his wisdom continues to shape how Matt thinks about nurturing potential in young people.

> *When given space to explore, children naturally reveal their authentic interests and capabilities.*

During their first practice, after basic warm-ups, the friend did something that seemed almost reckless at the time. Instead of running drills or assigning positions based on size and speed—the way most coaches would—he simply divided the players into two groups, explained the basic objective of getting the ball in the goal, and stepped back.

"Watch this," he said quietly, tossing the ball onto the field. "Take note of where each player naturally goes when they don't have specific instructions."

What unfolded was a revelation. Without being told where to play or what to do, each child naturally gravitated to their strengths. Some charged toward the ball, showing natural offensive instincts. Others hung back, intuitively protecting the goal. A few circled the action, processing the game at their own pace. Within minutes, Matt's friend had mapped out his roster. He has a list of clear offensive players, natural defenders, and several players who would need more focused attention to discover their natural talents. These were insights that hours of structured drills might never have revealed.

This moment transformed Matt's understanding not just of coaching, but also of parenting and education. After raising five athletic and active children—each involved in a whirlwind of activities, from violin to volleyball, chess to choir—he had seen a key principle play out countless times. When given space to explore, children naturally reveal their authentic interests and capabilities. Understandably, parents worry that it feels risky, even irresponsible, to step back and trust children to find their way. Won't they need constant direction? Won't they fall behind without strict guidance? What if they make mistakes or choose wrong? These fears are natural, but often unfounded. Research from the National Library of Medicine shows that children as young as seven demonstrate deep understanding of responsibility, and by age nine exhibit significant independent decision-making ability.[33] Yet, parents frequently stifle this natural development by overcrowding children's lives with instructions about what to do, when to do it, how to fix it, and what they did wrong.

Think about what Matt's friend did on that soccer field. He didn't abandon structure entirely; he created clear boundaries, explained the basic objective, and carefully observed what unfolded. The field had lines, the game had rules, but within those parameters, players had freedom to discover their natural roles. Similarly, we strive to find the delicate balance needed in education. We want to provide enough structure to guide the learner while leaving enough space for natural talents to emerge. The soccer team still needed coaches. Our children still need parents, teachers, mentors, and other caring adults to guide their journey. But, with an open education mindset, the parental role shifts from traffic director to careful observer and education designer, from controlling every action to creating meaningful opportunities. Instead of forcing children into predetermined positions, parents watch where they naturally gravitate and build from there.

Again, this is why our OpenEd company logo is a pair of parentheses or brackets. There's some kind of container, structure, or guardrails, but a lot of open space in between. The challenge lies in finding the right balance between guidance and independence.

> *The challenge lies in finding the right balance between guidance and independence.*

Unwind the Great Rewiring

Jonathan Haidt, a researcher and professor of social psychology at New York University, has diagnosed what he calls "the great rewiring of childhood."[34] This refers to the fundamental shift that occurred between 1980-2010 where society saw the gradual disappearance of "play-based childhood." Parents, driven by increasing fears about safety, began restricting children's independence and free movement. By 2010, what Haidt calls "phone-based childhood" had emerged, further reducing opportunities for genuine autonomy and real-world experience.

The consequences of this shift are profound. When children lack opportunities for independence and self-directed activity, they struggle to develop self-governance, or the ability to regulate their behavior, manage risks, and navigate social situations. His research through the Let Grow Project has shown that even small increases in childhood independence—like walking to school alone or running errands in the neighborhood—can significantly improve children's confidence and competence.

Psychology Professor Peter Gray has corroborated Haidt's research with his own studies of how children learn in non-coercive environments. In his 2013 book *Free to Learn: Why Unleashing the Instinct to Play Will Make Our Children Happier, More Self-Reliant, and Better Students for Life,* Gray relays how children are "designed by nature to educate themselves" through their innate drives of curiosity, playfulness, and sociability.[35] Yet in today's society, as we have observed firsthand, many children feel over-scheduled and over-controlled, rarely experiencing the kind of free play and exploration that Gray's research shows is crucial for development.

Gray identifies an important paradox, which is that the more we try to teach children in highly structured environments, the less they actually learn. His studies show that children in environments where they have significant autonomy—whether in democratic schools, homeschooling situations, or traditional societies—develop stronger problem-solving abilities and social skills than those in more controlled settings. The key isn't the absence of adults but rather their role as supporters and resources, not directors.

> *The more we try to teach children in highly structured environments, the less they actually learn.*

This research helps explain what Matt observed on the soccer field. When parents step back and let players naturally gravitate toward positions that interest them, they don't abandon their role as coaches. Instead, they are creating what Gray calls an "optimal learning environment"—one where children can explore and develop their abilities with supportive adults nearby, but who are not constantly directing their every move.

Don't be afraid that your child will make a mistake along their self-directed learning journey. Here's a reality check: your child *will* make mistakes. They will fail. But what is failure really, other than a learning opportunity? Their feelings will get hurt, and they might even hurt someone else's feelings. These experiences are part of life that cannot be avoided or prevented, nor should they be. When children have the opportunity to experience and endure these realities, they also have the opportunity to learn from them.

Parents are often held back by the fear that letting a child dive deep into one interest means they won't be well-rounded. But this fear is based on a misunderstanding about how humans actually develop capabilities. When Isaac worked with young people in Praxis, he noticed something fascinating. Whether they had spent their teens obsessively practicing violin, building computers, or running a lawn care business, the most successful participants all shared one crucial skill—they knew how to obsess over something. The deep dive into their passion hadn't just taught them about music or technology or entrepreneurship; it had taught them how to learn. This is vital in today's world of endless scrolling and fractured attention spans. A child who spends six months learning everything they can about dinosaurs is developing research skills, building focus, practicing how to find and evaluate information, and experiencing the thrill of genuine mastery. They don't just learn about dinosaurs, they learn how to master things deeply.

The ability to go deep on anything is becoming rare and valuable. Trying to make kids well-rounded through shallow exposure to many subjects often leaves them without any real mastery at all. They learn that knowledge is something to be briefly sampled and quickly forgotten after the test. But a child who has gone deep into even one topic knows what it feels like to truly understand something. That experience—knowing how to learn, focus, and achieve mastery—transfers to any new subject they choose to pursue. These kids enter the professional world and are the ones who most quickly adapt, learn technical jargon, workplace tools and norms, and specialized knowledge.

Most parents and educators get stuck when it comes to education by retreating to the safety of rigid control, assuming that giving children a voice in their education means abandoning structure altogether. These well-meaning adults understand on an intellectual level that children learn best when they have agency, the power to make meaningful choices about their learning. After all, it happens with games and toys. Yet, the fear that giving children agency equates to chaos stems from a fundamental misunderstanding. Consider again how brilliantly Minecraft works. Its players have complete agency to build anything they can imagine, but they must work within the game's physics, gather resources, and follow basic rules about how blocks connect. These constraints don't limit creativity, they enable it. The same principle applies to education.

Children who have agency in their learning don't need to abandon structure or academic rigor. Instead, they explore their interests deeply while acquiring fundamental skills in an environment that supports them. When children take the lead in their own education, they develop stronger critical thinking skills, greater intrinsic motivation, and perhaps most importantly, a deeper love for learning. They learn how to learn and practice choosing what they truly want to learn for themselves.

> *Children who have agency in their learning don't need to abandon structure or academic rigor.*

When Matt and Amy discovered this with their own family, it transformed how they thought about school choice. When their two youngest children reached 7th grade, Matt and Amy didn't simply default to sending them to the same flexible charter school their older siblings attended. Instead, they first had a conversation with their children about what they wanted and needed. Both chose the local district school (a decision that might seem counter to their belief in alternative education). The key wasn't where they went to school, it was that they had agency in the decision. During the inevitable mid-winter blues in February, when many students feel trapped, the conversation might have been quite different. "You chose this path," Matt and his wife Amy would remind them, "and you can choose differently next semester." This simple shift in framing transformed what could have felt like imprisonment into a challenge the kids owned.

Just as a child might combine LEGO pieces in unexpected ways, Matt's kids learned to mix and match educational approaches based on their needs. When one daughter (who likes math) was struggling with her school's new math curriculum, Matt and Amy didn't force her to push through or completely abandon her school. Instead, they crafted a hybrid solution. Their daughter chose homeschooling for just that one math period while continuing regular classes for everything else. The structured framework remained. With the flexibility to adapt where needed, she thrived.

Similarly, when Isaac and his family moved to Tennessee, their oldest was unsure what to do in a new place without his old friends. They were renting a house while they waited to move into their new place. It was summer, so they had only a few months to decide their education plans for the fall. Isaac brought his son to the coworking space he was using for work, booked a conference room, and pulled in a whiteboard. Isaac then asked his son to list his top three goals for the school year. What did he care most about? His list was:

1. Lots of time to hang out with friends
2. Ability to make money
3. Ability to play a sport

Pretty normal for a 16-year-old boy. Rather than judge these goals, or try to insist he include things like, "Get good grades," or "Learn valuable skills," Isaac took the goals at face value. Using these as a rubric to judge against, Isaac created three columns: public high school, private high school, and homeschooling/hybrid schooling. They ranked each on a scale of 1-5 based on how well they would likely allow or facilitate these three goals. His son ended up choosing public school for the fall semester. It didn't allow him time for a job and to earn money, but he felt it best allowed for goals one and three. He ran on the track team and met lots of new kids.

After one semester, Isaac's son grew restless and switched to homeschooling. He worked a lot of hours and saved a lot of money. He also joined the homeschool basketball team. Instead

> *Children who guide their own education develop stronger critical thinking skills, greater intrinsic motivation, and perhaps most importantly, a deeper love for learning.*

of Isaac trying to force his preferences on his son, or trying to force him to see which approach would best help him meet his own goals, Isaac presented him with tradeoffs. This way, he could see and weigh costs and benefits himself, take responsibility for his own learning journey, and discover what he truly valued.

This is what real educational agency looks like. It is not the absence of structure, but the power to make meaningful choices within a supportive framework. The irony is that many parents think sending their child to the default neighborhood school without discussion is the safe choice. In reality, that may be the true abdication of responsibility. Real structure comes from intentional conversations about goals, needs, and possibilities. The question isn't whether to provide structure, it's how to create the right kind of structure that enables rather than restricts.

Building Blocks of Agency: Love, Limits, and Latitude

Just as LEGO bricks can be combined to create increasingly complex structures, the larger building blocks of open education are sometimes made from smaller building blocks of their own. Within the framework we introduced earlier, giving your child voice requires its own foundational elements. Through our work with tens of thousands of families, we have discovered that a successful balance is most often achieved when built upon these three fundamental principles outlined in 2008 by Brigham Young University professors Craig H. Hart, Lloyd D. Newell, and Julie H. Haupt.[36] Like the standardized connections of LEGO bricks or the basic physics of Minecraft, these principles provide the foundation that makes meaningful choice possible. Many parents find that these concepts can provide a formula for joyful parenting itself:

1. Love
2. Limits
3. Latitude

Love means maintaining a kind, caring, and loving tone in every conversation about learning. It's about creating an environment where your child feels safe to explore, take risks, and sometimes fail. This doesn't mean empty praise, it means genuine support and understanding through the ups and downs of the learning journey.

Limits might seem counterintuitive when talking about educational freedom, but like a kite string, they're actually liberating. Clear boundaries help children feel secure enough to explore within them. Just as Minecraft's simple rules enable infinite creativity, well-defined limits give children the structure they need to thrive.

> *The key is maintaining enough structure for security while remaining flexible enough to adapt to changing circumstances.*

Latitude is about being willing to adjust. Life throws curveballs like health issues, financial challenges, or unexpected opportunities. Sometimes, those carefully crafted limits need to flex or shift temporarily. The key is maintaining enough structure for security while remaining flexible enough to adapt to changing circumstances.

The more you help your child own their educational decisions within this framework, the more they develop an individual sense of responsibility and love for learning, perhaps the greatest gift you can give them. Humans don't want hollow victories; we want to feel genuine success from tackling real challenges. This is where authentic learning happens. It's not in isolation, but in the messy integration of all life's elements working together.

The Science and Art of Play

For decades, educators and researchers viewed play as the opposite of learning. Play was considered a waste of time that needed to be limited in favor of serious education. But modern research has transformed this understanding, revealing play as one of the most natural and effective ways humans learn.

In 2017, the Peabody Essex Museum highlighted this shift with their groundbreaking "PlayTime" exhibition,

> "Enough time has passed since the bad old days of believing that play was a waste of time," declared their resident neuroscientist, Tedi Asher. "The cognitive benefits of play are too numerous to mention. Play can be a tool to socialize, play can help people build focus and increase brain size, and imaginative play can play a huge factor in building language skills."[37]

What Asher and other researchers discovered wasn't just that play could support learning, but that play might also be the most natural and effective way humans learn. The LEGO Foundation's research has since identified five key characteristics that make play-based learning so powerful:

1. **Joyful Learning:** When children genuinely enjoy their learning experience, their brains release neurochemicals that enhance memory formation and promote neural plasticity. Watch a child lost in creative play, whether they're building in Minecraft or constructing with physical blocks, and you'll see this principle in action.

2. **Meaningful Exploration:** Instead of memorizing isolated facts, children in play naturally integrate new information with what they already know. A child playing "restaurant" isn't just pretending, they're practicing math through making change, developing language skills through taking

orders, and building social understanding through role play. Each new concept connects to something real and relevant in their world.

3. **Active Engagement:** True learning requires being "minds-on," not just having hands-on engagement. In play, children naturally take ownership of their learning process. They are not passive recipients of information but active creators of understanding. This is why the most innovative companies like Google and Pixar create playful workspaces. They understand that breakthrough thinking requires the freedom to experiment.

4. **Iterative Discovery:** Watch a child building a LEGO tower. They try something, it falls, they adjust and try again. This natural cycle of hypothesis, test, and refinement is the foundation of both scientific thinking and entrepreneurial success. It's how SpaceX learned to land rockets and how startup founders find product-market fit.

5. **Social Interaction:** The most powerful learning happens in communities, especially with multi-age groups. Children naturally form groups in play, teaching and learning from each other. This doesn't stop in adulthood. From open-source software communities to makerspaces, the most innovative learning environments foster this same kind of collaborative play.

These principles also explain why some of the most successful companies in the world are moving away from rigid, traditional workplace structures. They are creating environments that look more like sophisticated playgrounds than conventional offices. When Google suggests engineers spend 20% of their time working on whatever interests them, or when Microsoft builds tree-house meeting spaces, they are attempting to apply these insights about how humans learn and create. Unfortunately, society postpones the myriad of opportunities to apply these principles until adulthood and instead forces children through a rigid, industrial-age education system, only to ironically spend millions redesigning workplaces to undo that conditioning later.

Giving children a voice in their education isn't about lowering standards or abandoning structure, it's about applying these proven principles of human learning and creativity from the start. When children are given meaningful agency in their learning journey, education is more enjoyable. They are better prepared for a world where the ability to direct their own learning, to experiment, fail, try again, collaborate, and create are the most valuable skills they can possess.

> *When children are given meaningful agency in their learning journey, education is more enjoyable.*

The LEGO Foundation's research reveals specific benefits that emerge when children have agency in their learning.[38] Among children aged 8-12, those who engaged in self-directed play-based learning showed 30% higher scores on creative problem-solving tasks. Even more striking, longitudinal studies found that students who experienced play-based learning environments were twice as likely to develop patents or start companies by age 30. In controlled studies across 49 countries, play-based learning consistently correlated with stronger executive function skills, better social development, and higher academic achievement, particularly in STEM fields.

When Concepts Meets Reality: Addressing Common Concerns

Parents often approach us with a mix of hope and anxiety. They see the research, they understand the principles, they are drawn to the idea of giving their children more voice in their education, but they have concerns. Let's address them head-on:

"**What about socialization?**" This is another backward concern. Traditional schools actually provide one of the most artificial social environments imaginable, segregating children strictly by birth year and forcing them to socialize only during designated periods. Children with more agency in their education often develop richer social skills because they interact with people of various ages in real-world contexts. They join community projects, participate in mixed-age learning groups, and engage with mentors in their areas of interest.

"**Won't my child fall behind academically?**" This fear gets things exactly backward. Think about any skill you've mastered as an adult. Did you learn it because someone forced you to study it for 45 minutes a day? Or did you learn it because you were genuinely interested and had the freedom to dive deep? When children have agency in their learning, they don't just keep up, they often go far beyond what traditional education expects. They learn to love learning itself.

"**What about college?**" Colleges are actively seeking students who can think independently and solve novel problems. The student who followed their passion for robotics through self-directed projects is far more interesting to admissions officers than someone who just checked all the standard boxes. More importantly, these students arrive at college knowing how to learn, not just how to follow instructions. Apart from that, the assumption that college is the ideal end for a K-12 graduate should come into question. Smart, ambitious kids are often ready to skip traditional college. (More on that later.)

"**They'll just play games all day!**" This objection reveals more about a parent's misconceptions than about children's capabilities. When given real agency—not just freedom from structure, but freedom within structure—children consistently surprise adults with their drive to tackle challenging projects and pursue meaningful work. The problem isn't that children just want to play. The problem is that the traditional education system has created a false dichotomy between play and learning.

"**They need to learn discipline.**" Perhaps the biggest misconception about giving children voice in their education is that it means letting them do whatever they want. But real discipline—the kind that serves kids throughout life—comes from pursuing challenging goals they actually care about. Watch a child spend hours perfecting their Minecraft architecture or debugging their first computer program. That's discipline. The difference is, it's driven by internal motivation rather than external pressure.

"My spouse and I already struggle with our children over homework. Won't this be worse?" Choosing to become education designers and adopt an open education mindset affects everyone in the family. It's important for both parents, including step-parents and divorced couples with joint custody, to openly share their thoughts, concerns, and ideas to make things work best for the child. Our experience indicates that when children have a voice in their education and are given the freedom to pursue their interests, the homework battles go away. Additionally, some parents find it works best to ask family members or join a co-op or microschool for support. Some save up to hire a retired teacher or young adult as a part-time helper during the week.

"They won't learn the basics." This might be the most ironic objection of all. Basic skills like reading, writing, and math are tools for pursuing interests and solving problems. When children have agency in their learning, they encounter these basics naturally and learn them more deeply because they see their practical value. A child pursuing a passion for dinosaurs will devour complex scientific texts far above their supposed reading level. A young entrepreneur selling crafts online will master percentages and profit margins without a single textbook.

The pattern here is clear. What parents typically fear most about giving children a voice in their education often turns out to be what delivers the best results. It's not that these concerns are irrational. They come from a real desire to see children succeed. However, they are based on an outdated model of what success looks like and how it's achieved.

What's missing is not conviction about giving children voice, it's understanding how to structure that voice for maximum impact. Elite athletes have long known that the most powerful growth happens not through constant grinding or complete freedom, but through focused sprints of intensive effort followed by periods of rest and recovery. This same insight, properly applied to education, transforms how children learn. In the next chapter, we'll explore how to structure learning sprints to harness your child's natural motivation and drive, creating the conditions where real growth happens.

> *Parents often approach us with a mix of hope and anxiety.*

CHAPTER 8 RECAP:

- Markus Persson, founder of Minecraft, understood something fundamental about human nature. He knew that when young people have true agency, deep learning happens.

- Building an open education mindset takes time. Let your children unwind. Help their brain reset from the daily grind of standardized schooling and gain a sense of independence in the process.

- The more we try to teach children in highly structured environments, the less they actually learn. The challenge lies in finding the right balance between guidance and independence.

- Parents are often held back by the fear that letting a child dive deep into one interest means they won't be well-rounded. The deep dive into their passion helps kids learn *how* to learn.

- The common concerns mentioned in the introduction are all addressed.

BUILDING BLOCK #5:
CELEBRATE LEARNER-DRIVEN SPRINTS

The Secrets of Pacing

Some of the world's best athletes have a secret that seems almost too simple to be true. They spend most of their time training at what feels like an embarrassingly easy pace. When exercise scientist Stephen Seiler first published this type of finding, the athletic community was skeptical. After all, doesn't peak performance come from constantly pushing your limits?

As Seiler dug deeper, he found this pattern everywhere he looked. Elite endurance athletes across multiple sports—from cross-country skiing to cycling to marathon running—spend about 80% of their training time at a surprisingly gentle intensity. They save the all-out effort for brief, focused periods that make up the remaining 20%. This polarized approach flies in the face of conventional wisdom. Most amateur athletes try to maintain a consistently challenging pace in every workout. But the pros know better. They understand that sustainable excellence comes from alternating between periods of foundation-building and intense focus. We see this same rhythm of excellence across many domains.

When Ken Thompson created the Unix operating system at Bell Labs in 1969, he didn't grind away at a steady pace. Instead, he worked in intense bursts—often coding for six to eight hours straight—followed by long walks to process and reflect. Ernest Hemingway wrote only in the early morning hours, stopping precisely at noon each day, having discovered that periods of intense focus followed by complete disengagement produced better work than constant effort.

We have found this same principle holds true in our own education and work. Life isn't one constant grind. It moves in natural cycles of focus and rest. The most successful companies use sprint cycles for major projects. Writers alternate between intense creative periods and extended inactive breaks. Even venture capital follows this pattern, with concentrated periods of deal evaluation followed by longer stretches of portfolio management.

Yet, the traditional education system often ignores these natural rhythms. Real learning happens in bursts of intense engagement, followed by essential periods of integration and reflection. Just like those elite athletes who discovered that constant, moderate effort isn't the path to excellence, marathon study sessions, cramming for tests, and rigid schedules often miss the mark.

It's Not About the Speed

For years, Isaac's oldest son's relationship with math was basically nonexistent. He has always been deeply analytical and philosophical, the kind of kid who would rather debate the existence of numbers than actually use them. At first, Isaac and his wife tried everything to help him develop a love for numbers. They used worksheets, games, and even bribes. Nothing worked. At various points, they attempted to impose structure and fought the daily battles that came with it. But in the end, they threw up their hands and decided to let him ignore math if he wanted to, telling him that he would need it eventually. He was unmoved.

Then, something unexpected happened. At age 13, he wanted to attend a two-day-a-week school program with his friends. The only hitch was that he needed to be at grade level in math. Suddenly, he had his own motivation to learn. He didn't care about math per se, but he wanted to attend this part-time school and not be embarrassed.

He said, "Okay, sign me up. I'll catch up with math this summer before the semester starts."

Given his past, Isaac was skeptical. He offered to help, but his son declined, saying, "I'll just jump on Khan Academy and start at kindergarten level."

Isaac was impressed that his son had no fear or shame of being 13 years old and starting with kindergarten math. All he cared about was catching up, and he figured it would be easier if he started from absolute scratch. In less than three months and spending only about an hour or two per day, this math-hating teenager completed nine grades of math curriculum and caught up to his peers. Not because his parents forced him, but because he had found his own reason to learn. He was no math whiz, but he knew it well enough to get decent grades and not feel stupid around his friends. Isaac was astounded. Instead of suffering through nearly a decade of daily torture, his son skipped it all and then caught up in one massive sprint with little pain. Parents don't worry so much about their kids being behind when they know how easy it is for them to progress a tremendous amount in a short sprint.

When Isaac shared this story with a former colleague Hannah Frankman, founder of Rebel Educator, she offered an additional insight. While she sees many families discovering that core subjects can often be covered in much less time than traditional schooling requires, she emphasizes that speed shouldn't be the goal in itself. As Hannah said, "The point isn't to turn education into some kind of academic sprint where we're racing to finish algebra or chemistry as quickly as possible. The real opportunity is what opens up when we free ourselves from rigid schedules—the space for genuine interests to flourish, for deep projects to unfold, for real learning to happen."

She's absolutely right. Isaac's son's math story isn't about academic acceleration or bragging rights. It's about finding the right motivation at the right time. Some kids will zip through certain subjects when they're ready and motivated. Others will take their time, developing deep understanding at a slower pace. Both approaches are perfectly valid. Trees don't grow at a steady pace throughout the year. They alternate between periods of intense growth in spring and summer, followed by essential rest and consolidation in fall and winter. Our brains tend to follow this pattern.

A learning sprint isn't about speed. It's about creating a container for natural learning to flourish. A sprint is a focused period where your child can dive deep into something that genuinely interests them, supported by a simple structure that helps maintain momentum without imposing artificial pressure.

> *A learning sprint isn't about speed.*

In previous chapters, we've explored how to identify your child's unique needs, map available resources, and give them a meaningful voice in their education. Now we're ready to take all those insights and transform them into something practical. We'll share a framework for action that will give you a quick win and the momentum and confidence to continue your own personalized education design journey. It's called the learner-driven sprint.

The Anatomy of a Sprint

A learner-driven sprint is a two-week adventure where your child gets to dive deep into something that genuinely interests them. But unlike those endless school projects that seem to drag on forever, these sprints have a simple structure that keeps things moving while leaving room for creativity and discovery.

The fascinating thing about learning sprints is how they align with what brain scientists have discovered about how we actually learn. Think about the last time you really mastered something new, whether learning to play guitar, figuring out a new software program, or rock climbing. Chances are, you didn't progress at a steady, predictable pace. Instead, you probably experienced bursts of intense focus and progress, followed by periods where things needed to settle. That's your brain's natural learning rhythm at work. It's like building muscle. Your muscles get stronger during the recovery period *after* the workout. The same principle applies to learning. The two-week time frame provides enough space for both intense focus and essential integration of new knowledge, mapping perfectly to the brain's natural learning patterns.

The sprint structure is elegantly simple, built around three key connection points shown in this "Learner-driven Sprints" tool:

LEARNER-DRIVEN SPRINTS

Launch Chat (10 minutes)
- Review chosen focus areas
- Identify needed resources
- Set clear goals for two weeks ahead

Mid-Sprint Check-in (5 minutes to 1 hour)
- Review progress
- Address any obstacles
- Adjust course if needed

Sprint Celebration Night (30 minutes)
- Share what was learned
- Receive family feedback
- Reflect on next steps

The magic starts even before the first meeting. Remember those lists you created in a previous chapter with your child's interests, needs, and available resources? This is where they come alive. Help your child identify three to five key points they want to explore during the sprint. Maybe they're fascinated by ancient Egypt, or perhaps they want to learn how to code their own video game. The topic isn't what matters. What matters is that they are choosing it, and they can tell you why.

Launch day is simple. Schedule a quick 10 minute meeting to map out the journey ahead. What resources will they need? Who might be able to help? Sometimes these conversations spark even more excitement than the project itself.

Halfway through—one week in—you should pause for a check-in. How's it going? Any obstacles? Need to adjust course? For some families, these meetings last five minutes ("Everything's great, Dad!"), and for others, they turn into hour-long conversations about hieroglyphics or JavaScript. That's the beauty of it. Just follow the energy.

Finally, the sprint culminates in a celebration of learning. This isn't your typical school presentation; it's more like a mini-festival of discovery. Your child might present in any of the following ways:

- Demonstrate a scientific experiment
- Share a video they created
- Show off a board game they designed
- Launch a simple website
- Present a mini-magazine with photos and articles
- Host an art gallery or meme collection
- Host a screening for their stop-motion animation film

With an open education mindset, keep any sprint assessment simple with the "mastered or not yet" framework mentioned earlier in this book. Instead of grading the work, look for two things: 1) did the project yield at least three new insights? and 2) does the final presentation reflect meaningful engagement with the topic? If a key topic or skill needs more work, let the learner choose to refine and present again later, or take the feedback forward into their next sprint.

These celebrations matter more than you might think. One of the key mindset shifts in open education is learning to celebrate both the victories and the setbacks; yes, even the failures. Some families call these gatherings "showcase nights," while others prefer names like "sprint finales" or "ed-ventures." The name of the showcase night isn't nearly as important as making the celebration a regular part of your family culture.

> *The name of the showcase night isn't nearly as important as making the celebration a regular part of your family culture.*

Start simple, then let these celebrations evolve with your family's style. Matt and his family began with basic conversations around the dinner table, but over time, they grew into something more. They rotated hosting duties among family members, including special refreshments (somehow brownies and ice cream make everything more festive). If interested, they would sometimes share their projects with grandparents and cousins via email or video chat. Depending on your family's schedule, you could do monthly showcase nights. Some align them with seasons of the year or with natural learning rhythms. There's no right way, just what works well for your crew.

Favorite project creations, presentations, or a highlighted piece of work can be saved in what some call the "journey journal," "a learning log," or "portfolio of work." This is a mix of physical and digital collections that highlight each child's growth. It's amazing to watch kids flip through their old projects, seeing how far they've come. These portfolios become more than just memories, they're proof of capability, creativity, and perseverance. When college applications or job opportunities come around, these collections can tell a powerful story about who your child is and what they can do.

Learning Sprints in Action: Kai's Story

Kai stood in front of his "Poisonous Forest Creatures" presentation, fingers drumming against his leg. Three months ago, he would have rather hidden in his room than show his work to anyone. But something about these two-week sprints had clicked for him in a way that years of traditional assignments never had.

"Ready, honey?" Maya asked, adjusting the refreshments on the table. They had made it a family tradition to have snacks at these sprint finales. Tonight it was pizza, Kai's choice for his first mastered project.

"I think so," Kai said, glancing at his notes one last time. "But isn't Uncle Ethan coming, too?"

"Wouldn't miss it," came the reply from the doorway. Uncle Ethan was already helping himself to a slice. "I've been looking forward to learning about these forest creatures of yours.

Maya watched her son take a deep breath, the way he always did before tackling something new. The transformation he'd made in just three months still amazed her. She remembered that first conversation about trying sprints. Kai curled up in his usual spot on the window seat, skepticism written all over his face.

"Two weeks?" he asked. "That's all?"

"That's all," she'd assured him. "And we'll check in halfway through to see how it's going."

"And if it's not perfect?"

"Then it's 'not yet' mastered. We adjust and keep moving."

Something about that simple framework had unlocked a hidden curiosity in Kai. Maybe it was knowing there was a clear endpoint. Maybe it was the freedom to choose his own topic. Or maybe it was just the pizza.

"Okay everyone," Kai said now, standing a little straighter. "I've been researching poisonous creatures that live in our local forests. Did you know there are 14 different species within 10 miles of our house?"

Maya caught Marcus's eye across the room. Their son, who used to freeze up during class presentations, was now launching into a detailed explanation of newt neurotoxins. The same boy who could barely sit still for 15 minutes was now leading his family through a carefully organized presentation, complete with hand-drawn illustrations and a map of local sightings. When he finished, the questions started flowing. Isabella wanted to know more about the chemical properties of the toxins. Ava was curious about which trails to avoid while hiking. Even Uncle Ethan had detailed questions about snake identification.

"And look," Kai said, pulling out his project journal. "I tracked everything I learned." He had created a simple chart with green checkmarks for mastered concepts and yellow circles for things he was still figuring out. No red marks, no failing grades, just a clear record of progress.

Maya remembered Olivia's words from months ago when she said, "The magic is in giving kids a container small enough to feel manageable, but big enough to do something meaningful."

Looking at Kai now, proudly answering questions about his forest creatures, Maya could see exactly what her friend had meant. These sprints weren't about racing through material or checking off requirements. They were about creating space for genuine learning to unfold at exactly the right pace.

"Mom?" Kai's voice brought her back to the present. "Can my next sprint be about teaching other kids about forest safety? Mrs. Chen said I could do a presentation for the younger grades."

Maya smiled. From hiding in his room to planning classroom presentations, all because they had found a way to make learning feel possible again.

"Of course," she said. "Let's start planning tomorrow."

CHAPTER 9 RECAP:

- When we free ourselves from rigid schedules, genuine interests flourish, deep projects unfold, and real learning happens.
- The two-week timeframe of a sprint provides enough space for both intense focus and essential integration of new knowledge, mapping perfectly to the brain's natural learning patterns.
- Start with a Launch Chat (10 minutes), followed by a Mid-Sprint Check-in (5 minutes to 1 hour), and concluding with a Sprint Celebration Night! (30 minutes). Start simple, then let these celebrations evolve with your family's style.

PART III

CHAPTER 10:

OPEN EDUCATION PATHWAYS AFTER HIGH SCHOOL

Real Life Teaching

When we talk to parents about their children's future, there's understandably a lot of worry of the unknown. They want their kids to succeed, to find fulfilling careers, to thrive in an increasingly complex world. But there's a gnawing fear that the traditional path—the one most of us were told to follow— might not be enough anymore. And you know what? That fear is justified.

Imagine if we taught kids to ride a bike the way we prepare them for life after high school. We would start by showing them pictures of bikes when they're young, have them memorize parts and traffic rules, write essays about famous cyclists, and maybe let them sit on a stationary bike once in a while. Then, after 12+ years of this bike education, we would expect them to hop on a real bicycle and ride flawlessly through rush-hour traffic. Sounds absurd, right? Yet, this is precisely how we often approach career preparation for most young people today. This bicycle analogy captures the disconnect between the traditional education system and the real world. But this analogy only scratches the surface of our current predicament.

Imagine if, on top of their inadequate preparation, these novice cyclists were thrust onto a highway—a more advanced pathway where they are expected to perform at their peak, that we'll call the job market—where the rules had suddenly changed. The speed limits have been removed, lane markers constantly shift, and traffic signals malfunction regularly. Even experienced drivers would struggle to navigate this new terrain. This is the reality of our 21st-century job market. In this fast-changing landscape, closed education is falling woefully short. The skills that were once considered essential are quickly becoming obsolete. Meanwhile, entirely new industries and job categories are emerging faster than our educational institutions can adapt. It's not just about learning to ride a bike anymore, it's about learning to ride a bike that's transforming beneath you, on a road that's constantly changing its course.

Record numbers of college graduates remain underemployed or working in fields unrelated to their studies. Many are drowning in student loan debt, with no clear path to the financial stability they were promised. At the same time, employers are struggling to find candidates with the right mix of skills and adaptability to thrive in this new environment. It's clear that our approach to preparing young people for the future needs a radical rethink. This rethink is already underway, driven by both necessity and innovation.

Mike Rowe, the host of the TV show *Dirty Jobs*, known for his advocacy of skilled trades and industry-relevant certifications, pointed out a stark reality when he noted that 50% of people who start a college pursuit don't finish.[39] These individuals often end up with the worst of both worlds; substantial debt and no degree to show for it. Even among those who do graduate, the picture isn't much brighter.

According to recent data, a staggering 62% of college graduates either have no job or are working in positions that don't require a degree.[40] In response to this mismatch between education and employment, there is a rise in alternative credentialing and skills-based hiring. Data from the National Student Clearinghouse Research Center shows that enrollment in vocational community colleges has jumped 16% since 2018, as more young people seek practical, job-ready skills. This shift isn't just happening on the education side; employers are changing too. Major companies like IBM, Accenture, Dell, Bank of America, and Google have started dropping college degree requirements for many positions, focusing instead on candidates' actual skills and abilities. An IBM executive once said that he would rather hire a failed entrepreneur than an MBA. Why? Because entrepreneurs, regardless of their formal education, have developed crucial problem-solving skills and adaptability. They've learned to see the world differently, to identify opportunities where others see obstacles.

> *An IBM executive once said that he would rather hire a failed entrepreneur than an MBA.*

Entrepreneurship Inspires Learning

Matt once chatted with a young man in his early twenties flying to California from New York. Matt asked him what he did for a living and the man replied, "I'm the CFO for my band." Matt inquired where he learned to manage finances and the young man said, "Selling stuff on the street. I learned quickly how important margins are to making money. I did it well, so my band put me in charge of finances."

When he learned about how OpenEd helps young people think differently about education, he provided Matt with one of the most profound (and practical) responses Matt had ever heard. The young man said, "I wish someone would have told me there were other options than just chasing credits in high school and then going to college. My high school counselor told me I would be a failure if I didn't go to college. I told her I didn't see the ROI (return on investment) for paying such steep tuition for classes I didn't want to take. I shared with her that it simply didn't make sense to go into massive debt and maybe get a job where I could afford to pay off the debt. No thanks, I told her," the young man said. "I'll just go make money on my own. So that's what I'm doing now and I'm loving it."

Entrepreneurs are on the front lines of identifying ways to innovate, adapt, and create value in a rapidly changing world. These are the skills that are needed in today's job market, often more so than the book credentials listed on a transcript gained from earning a diploma. For an increasing number of young people, entrepreneurship is a way to build confidence, leadership skills, and essential learning pathways outside of traditional schooling.

As any entrepreneur will tell you, the experience of starting a business is an emotional rollercoaster. It is filled with highs and lows and provides the entrepreneur with an endless list of opportunities to evaluate, markets to pursue, decisions to make, and problems to solve. It can be exhilarating! The experience is also extremely educational. Just like trees need strong winds to grow deep roots and muscles need heavy weights to become strong, the learning that is generated through the challenges of entrepreneurship provides some of the most deeply gained knowledge and skills ever imagined. A famous slogan from Nike applies to learning as well as entrepreneurship: "No pressure. No diamonds." Each of us needs meaningful challenges to grow and expand our capabilities.

Open education, with its emphasis on real-world experience and self-directed learning, creates natural pathways for entrepreneurial development. Unlike traditional closed education systems that focus on standardized curricula and predetermined outcomes, open education encourages students to:

- Identify and pursue opportunities based on their interests and market needs
- Learn through direct experience and controlled risk-taking
- Develop skills in real-time response to actual challenges

- Build networks and relationships outside the classroom walls
- Create value before receiving credentials

This approach mirrors the entrepreneurial journey itself. Entrepreneurship, with its inherent uncertainties and challenges, provides an ideal environment for developing strong and confident learners.

Start with Why

In his influential work, *Start with Why*, Simon Sinek introduces the concept of the "Golden Circle," emphasizing the importance of understanding the *why* behind our actions. This principle is particularly relevant when considering education and career planning.[41]

Too often, students pursue degrees or career paths without a clear understanding of their purpose. They focus on the what (getting a degree) or the how (attending classes, passing exams), without considering the fundamental *why* that should drive their choices. As Sinek explains, "People don't buy what you do; they buy why you do it."[42] In the context of education, this means that success isn't just about accumulating knowledge or credentials, but it's about aligning your learning journey with your core values and aspirations.

For students embracing an open education mindset, this means asking deeper questions:

- Why am I pursuing this particular path of study?
- How does this align with my personal goals and values?
- What impact do I want to make in the world?

By starting with *why*, students can make more intentional choices about their education and career paths. This approach leads to greater engagement, motivation, and ultimately,

> *By starting with why, students can make more intentional choices about their education and career paths.*

success. Through this lens, we can see that entrepreneurship isn't just about starting businesses, it's about fostering crucial skills for success in any field.

By incorporating entrepreneurial projects into the learning journey, we can help students develop:

- **Self-directed, continuous curiosity:** Successful entrepreneurs embrace curiosity. They are always striving to acquire new knowledge and skills to solve important problems. This habit of lifelong learning is invaluable in our rapidly changing world.
- **Problem-solving:** Every business faces unique challenges. Entrepreneurial projects teach students to think creatively and find innovative solutions.
- **Resilience:** Failure is an inherent part of entrepreneurship and life. Learning to bounce back from setbacks builds the resilience needed for long-term success.
- **Interdisciplinary thinking:** Running a business requires cross-disciplinary knowledge of finance, marketing, communication, operations, and more. This holistic approach contrasts sharply with the siloed nature of traditional subject-based education.

A powerful example of entrepreneurship in education is the story of Aiden Prout, a student who participated in the OpenEd program from ages 5-18. Aiden started a business at age 17 focused on building weed-free and water-efficient garden boxes. Aiden's entrepreneurial pursuit started in 2021 with the thought-provoking question of "What would happen if growing healthy food could be done with less work, less water, and no weeding ever?" This question led him to develop an innovative solution that would revolutionize home gardening.

Using 3D modeling skills learned in an OpenEd course, Aiden began product development while still in high school. He quickly gained practical experience in market research, product iteration, and customer feedback. The importance of failing fast and adapting to market needs became clear as he reiterated his product three times in the first four months based on real sales and customer feedback. Aiden's solution offers a fresh perspective on an expensive gardening method. While multi-million-dollar indoor hydroponics systems are out of reach for most gardeners, Aiden developed a way to grow outdoors using the sun, less water, no electric pumps, and minimal time and effort. His product appeals to both first-time gardeners seeking an easy green thumb and seasoned gardeners looking for low-maintenance, water-efficient solutions.

The results were astounding. In just 12 months, Aiden earned over $150,000, far exceeding his initial goal of $10,000. His success not only demonstrates the potential of student entrepreneurship but also addresses real-world issues such as water scarcity in dry climates. This hands-on approach to learning goes beyond theoretical knowledge. As Aiden puts it, "The things you learn when you create a real business are not in textbooks. They're things you experience firsthand." Aiden's story, which can be explored further at WeedFreeGarden.com, serves as an inspiration to other students and a testament to the effectiveness of OpenEd's approach to education.

Again, not every student needs to be an entrepreneur for life. However, we strongly encourage everyone to start a business at some point and strive to think like an entrepreneur throughout their lives. At a minimum, every young person ought to spend time practicing how to market themselves starting with *why* before working their way to the *what* and the *how*. Of course, the *what* and the *how* still matter in education. For those who determine that college is the right path, it's crucial to approach it with clear eyes. Students need to carefully consider how higher education facilitates their objectives, enhances their skills, and expands their networks. However, this consideration must be balanced against the significant costs and time commitments.

The financial reality of higher education in the 21st century is too stark to ignore. According to the Federal Reserve, the average student debt reached a staggering $37,000 in 2024.[43] But this figure only tells part of the story. Almost two-thirds of college graduates either work at a job unrelated to their college major, or their job does not require a degree at all, raising serious questions about the return on investment of a college education for many students. Therefore, it has become essential for parents and students to explore alternatives to an expensive college education that might offer better value.

One parent shared with Matt an enlightening story that illustrates this point perfectly. Their teenage daughter, demonstrating remarkable foresight, carefully compared the curriculum for both a high school diploma and an associate degree. Her astute analysis led her to a surprising conclusion. She discovered that the associate degree was essentially a repeat of high school. Instead of resigning herself to this redundancy, this young woman took charge of her education. At just 15 years old, she opted to take competency-based college courses online. While still participating in high school activities and maintaining her social life, she focused on college-level work. She completed most of her associate degree before finishing high school, gaining not just credits but the confidence to take charge of her own education. Early college programs have emerged as an innovative educational model to effectively bridge the gap between high school and higher education, providing motivated (or simply practical) students with a significant head start on their college careers. By allowing students to earn credits early, these programs can shorten the time and reduce the overall cost of obtaining a college degree.

Southern New Hampshire University (SNHU-CBE) and OpenEd

A prime example of such a program is the partnership between Southern New Hampshire University (SNHU-CBE) and OpenEd, which offers high school students the chance to earn a college degree through a self-paced, online program. Participants enroll in SNHU's competency-based (CBE) associate or bachelor's degree programs through OpenEd. All courses are offered online, allowing students to learn at their own pace and balance their studies with other commitments. Unlike traditional college models, the program employs an interdisciplinary, project-based learning approach with transparent rubrics and a "mastered or not yet" grading system. Students can complete as many credits as they want within a 16-week term, allowing ambitious learners to accelerate their education. At a fraction of the cost of traditional college, the program offers exceptional financial value.

> *At a fraction of the cost of traditional college, the program offers exceptional financial value.*

Beyond the financial advantages, the competency-based model ensures students gain practical, applicable skills that translate directly to the workplace. This focus on real-world skills can give students a competitive edge as they enter the job market. Students receive personalized support through one-on-one coaching and mentoring from OpenEd staff, ensuring they have the guidance needed to succeed.

The program offers a range of degree options to suit various career aspirations, including in business, healthcare, communications, and more. Students who enroll in SNHU-CBE through OpenEd typically have no illusions about their degree being their sole ticket to success. Yes, it signals a concrete skill set that can open the door to an interview or job promotion, but any degree is simply one small part of a professional's overall portfolio.

Employers are increasingly looking for candidates who possess a diverse array of skills that go beyond traditional academic knowledge. Owen Fuller, CEO of Marq, a fast-growing tech startup, recently told his team to look for **demonstrated excellence**

in any area for the candidates they are interviewing. When parents, teachers, and other caring adults help young people find ways to demonstrate excellence in areas they are passionate about, those students are better prepared for future job interviews or entrepreneurial pitch moments.

The World Economic Forum's "Future of Jobs Report 2023" highlights the top skills employers expect to be increasingly important by 2027:[44]

- Analytical thinking
- Creative thinking
- Resilience, flexibility, and agility
- Motivation and self-awareness
- Curiosity and lifelong learning

Notably, these skills are not tied to any specific field or degree, but are universally valuable across industries. This shift underscores the need for students to develop a broad skill set that complements their core academic knowledge.

While academic knowledge provides a crucial foundation, supplementing it with practical, real-world skills is essential. This could involve internships, part-time jobs, volunteer work, or personal projects. For instance, a computer science student might complement their coursework by contributing to open-source projects or building their own apps. This hands-on experience not only reinforces academic learning but also provides tangible evidence of skills for future employers. Soft skills, often overlooked in traditional education, are increasingly valued by employers. Communication—both written and verbal—leadership, teamwork, adaptability, and time management are key soft skills that can only be developed

> *While academic knowledge provides a crucial foundation, supplementing it with practical, real-world skills is essential.*

through group projects, extracurricular activities, or leadership roles in student organizations.

Finally, in an age of artificial intelligence and automation, uniquely human skills like creativity and critical thinking are more valuable than ever. Students need hands-on training in interdisciplinary learning. They need to practice problem-solving with complex, open-ended challenges, embrace failure as a learning opportunity, and pursue creative hobbies born of passion not compulsion. Students also need to learn how to showcase these skills through concrete examples. Rather than simply listing "creativity" or "problem solving" on a resumé, OpenEd students are encouraged to create a portfolio of their work showing highlights of their experiences. This portfolio might include project write-ups, case studies, or even video presentations demonstrating their skills in action. At OpenEd, we strongly encourage students to create a personal website or blog to showcase their best work. Each project should tell a story answering questions such as "What was the challenge? How did you approach it? What were the results?"

We are big believers in students doing what we call "working out loud"—sharing their learning process and insights as they go. This could mean students regularly posting on LinkedIn key updates about projects they tackle, challenges they overcome, or new skills they develop. Students often think that networking is just about who they know. More than this, it's about how they are perceived by those they know. And even more than that, it's about how they can apply what they know to the problems those connections are looking to solve. This is how students show their value to potential employers, clients or partners, and this is the key to career success in a competitive landscape.

> *We are big believers in students doing what we call "working out loud"—sharing their learning process and insights as they go.*

Alternative Paths to Success: What's Old is New Again

Throughout much of history, formal education requirements were not the norm for most professions. Skills were typically learned through apprenticeships and on-the-job training. The rise of standardized education and degree requirements is a relatively recent phenomenon. Now, there is a shift back toward skills-based hiring, with many employers valuing demonstrated abilities over formal credentials.

Mike Rowe and others have brought attention to the overlooked opportunities in blue collar jobs. Ironically, modern blue collar workers are often higher skilled and higher earning than their office-dwelling counterparts. Some have used the term "new collar jobs" to better reflect the ever-changing landscape of the modern economy. As Rowe puts it, "America is lending money we don't have, to kids who can't pay it back, to train them for jobs that no longer exist."[45]

Where's the logic in that? Meanwhile, he points to a smoldering crater in our workforce where the vocational arts once stood in high schools. According to the U.S. Chamber of Commerce, over 10 million jobs remained unfilled as of February 2024, many in skilled trades and technical fields.[46]

CTE—or Career and Technical Education—has become a buzzword in the education world. In fact, over the past 20 years, media mentions of CTE have increased noticeably. It's a movement that is long overdue in a country where parents and guidance counselors have been pushing a misguided "college for all" narrative for far too long. While society has been busy steering kids toward four-year degrees, Rowe has been shining a spotlight on entrepreneurs like the pork farmer he met on the program *Dirty Jobs* who pulls in a cool $200,000 a year. As Rowe puts it, "We need to make work cool again."[47]

> *"We're lending money we don't have, to kids who can't pay it back, to train them for jobs that no longer exist."*
> —*Mike Rowe*

This means celebrating the essential skills that keep our society running, from the construction trades, like plumbing and electrical, to healthcare and advanced manufacturing.

Still, a majority of high schoolers have no idea what CTE stands for, let alone consider it for their own careers. CTE programs are evolving to bridge this gap, offering students hands-on experience in high-demand areas like healthcare, IT, welding, and advanced manufacturing. These aren't your old-timer's shop classes. Modern CTE encompasses a wide range of disciplines, and students can often earn industry certifications alongside their high school diploma, giving them a head start in their careers. Programs like SkillsUSA host annual national competitions where tens of thousands of students showcase their skills in everything from welding to robotics. Moreover, CTE is evolving with technology. Curriculum programs like Victory XR are integrating virtual and augmented reality to give students an immersive taste of jobs like welding or machining, without the associated physical risks that novices typically face.

The challenge now is to align our 21st-century education system with the realities of this "new collar" job market and create a more flexible, responsive education system that prepares students for the jobs that actually exist. Some states are taking notice. Florida, for example, now recognizes various coding and web development certifications as part of their career education funding.[48] For parents and students, embracing CTE doesn't mean abandoning traditional academics. Many districts offer CTE programs or partner with technical schools. At OpenEd, we advise parents to encourage their children to participate in hands-on projects or summer programs that align with their interests.

Due to our belief that CTE is a critical aspect of education, OpenEd students have access to a number of industry-leading programs, courses, curricula, and related certifications—often at no cost to the family. Visit opened.co to learn more.

Many people acknowledge that traditional, academic college may not be a great path for those going into the skilled trades or blue / new collar careers. That is undoubtedly true. But this acknowledgment often completely misses another huge population for whom college is largely a waste of time and money. It's the young adults who are pursuing the growing number of jobs that don't require a degree.

Isaac has personally seen and helped hundreds of young people who have no degree or experience win white-collar jobs that supposedly required a degree (more on that below). There is an idea that, for those less intelligent or ambitious, college may not be worth it, but it is for the smartest and most ambitious. This is false. In fact, when you consider what a degree signals to some observers—this degree holder is likely as good as all other similar degree holders—you realize that degrees are a particularly bad deal for those with above average intelligence and ambition, because it makes them look average. It's a lot easier than you think to create a better signal of your knowledge, capability, and creativity, as we will explore shortly.

But what about the experience of college? If what you really want is the social experience or the classroom experience, move to a college town and attend everything without paying tuition. They almost assuredly won't kick you out!

The proliferation of alternative career paths and the growing recognition of skills-based hiring will correctly lead many students and parents to conclude that college is not necessary for success. This conclusion often leads students and parents to logically wonder if an official high school diploma is essential for success. It's worth noting that, while Isaac has multiple college degrees (which he does not value, but that's a separate point), he never got a high school diploma. He recently received an email from a parent, Joanna, who was grappling with this very dilemma:

I would love resources about college after homeschool/ online school. My child completed 9th grade last year on the traditional district diploma path, but we are now planning to pursue an alternative diploma path this year. My child needs options and more flexibility than we felt were available on the official district diploma path. However, I worry a lot about not following the traditional 'earn a district diploma and then go to college' path. I would love help specific to college and/or other training when doing school through OpenEd.

For context, students in the OpenEd program are given two options: an official, accredited district diploma or an OpenEd certificate of completion. The district diploma includes specific state and district credit requirements resulting in the exact same credential that a traditional high school graduate would receive. The certificate path is for students and parents who choose to place a higher value on self-directed learning and flexibility. Over the years, the vast majority of OpenEd families choose the flexibility of the certificate over the official district diploma. Either way, every student can still pursue whatever post-high school pathway they desire.

Back to this parent's question. Many parents struggle with this decision, as society has pushed a linear path to success for over a hundred years: high school diploma → college degree → good job → retirement = success.

But as education and work evolve, so must the approach to preparing kids for the future. A fact that many people don't realize is that a high school diploma is no longer required to go to college, nor does it guarantee success in a career. Contrary to common fears, a non-traditional high school path doesn't close these doors either. Colleges and universities increasingly recognize the value of diverse experiences and skills that students from alternative educational backgrounds bring to their campuses. Most (if not all) colleges now offer some form of open enrollment and, if no official district diploma is available to submit, the admission offices typically provide an option to submit portfolios, essays, or well-documented homeschool transcripts. As we have already covered, what matters more is demonstrating readiness for college-level work.

Here is how some successful non-traditional students have done it:

- **Build a compelling portfolio**: Maintain detailed records of all educational activities, projects, and achievements.

- **Leverage early college credits**: Programs like Southern New Hampshire University's competency-based education offer college credits to high school students through community partners.

- **Standardized tests**: If your student has focused on learning the skill of taking tests, many colleges still accept scores on the SAT or ACT scores as a demonstration of preparedness.

- **Embrace your uniqueness**: Colleges often value soft skills, like discipline and time management, just as much as academic prowess.

But what if traditional college isn't the goal? The beautiful part of the flexible path beyond a district diploma is that it opens up a world of alternatives:

- **Vocational training**: Programs in culinary arts, cybersecurity, and more, offer hands-on learners direct paths to lucrative careers.

- **Apprenticeships**: Many industries, especially trades, provide paid apprenticeships leading to stable, well-paying careers.

- **Entrepreneurship**: Starting a business, like Olivia's dog breeding venture, can be a viable alternative to college with the right skills and mindset.

- **Gap-year programs**: Structured gap years provide valuable life experience and help clarify future goals.

The definition of what we used to call a traditional education or career path is becoming increasingly fluid. The key to adopting an open education mindset is to align educational choices with individual talents, interests, and goals, whether that happens in a classroom, online, through an apprenticeship, or via self-directed projects. Our current education system often dispenses years of abstract content *at* students, leaving them ill-equipped for the real world. Instead, education should be viewed like teaching someone to ride a bike. Start with training wheels, gradually increase challenges, and celebrate the inevitable scrapes and falls as valuable learning experiences.

Similarly, aspiring entrepreneurs should practice small and simple steps with any business idea. As they progress, they learn what customers want, how to message it to them, what price point works well, and in the process manage how to handle rejection, feedback, and complaints. These are skills needed for small enterprises as well as multi-million dollar businesses. No one is expected to run a business that generates significant income without developing these basic skills first. Practice helps any entrepreneur become better prepared for when one of their ideas finally makes it big time.

So, is pursuing entrepreneurship better than a college degree? Depending on the young adult's goal, Isaac and Matt would likely say "Yes!"

"Burn your resumé." Isaac told this to a group of young people who were looking for their first job. They stared blankly for a minute, waiting to see if he was joking. He wasn't. After helping thousands of people get their first real job, he knew what worked and his advice was dead serious. To make it less scary, he posed a question, "If you didn't have the ability to send a resumé or cover letter, what would you send?"

Often, job seekers think their resumé, and the bullets on it, are a strong signal to employers of their value. But it's an increasingly weak signal. "BA in Business from Generic State U" doesn't communicate anything about your ability. In fact, it only signals that you are likely to be no worse than the average degree holder from that institution. Isaac had this realization in college as he looked around at all the hungover kids in class and wondered if that was what he was buying, a piece of paper that says he's probably no worse than the rest.

The good news is, building a better signal of one's value is easier than ever. We have seen hundreds of young people, as young as seventeen, with no degree, no diploma, no standard test scores, and no experience win jobs that supposedly required a bachelor's degree and three years of experience. How? By building a better signal of their value. By being their own credential. They researched companies and hiring managers, created projects, landing pages, or pitch decks, sent emails with custom video cover letters, and even offered to do free work to prove themselves. This method landed an interview for every three pitches sent, and a job offer for every seven, and took an average of just five weeks to get that offer. Contrast that with the typical approach of attaching standard resumes and cover letters to applications, which, according to employment surveys and the Bureau of Labor Statistics, takes an average of 85 applications and six and a half months to get an offer.

> *The good news is, building a better signal of one's value is easier than ever.*

When employers see something more interesting than grades, diplomas, and degrees, they place less emphasis on education and more on the outcomes demonstrated by a project, pitch, or apprenticeship. All of these are vastly better signals of someone's ability to create value than a mere resumé. In fact, the two things that often matter the most when determining whether someone will succeed in their career: 1) ability to create value for others (skills); and 2) ability to prove it (signal).

Education should be about discovering and developing what you enjoy (or don't hate), what you are reasonably good at (or not terrible at), and what other people will pay you for and then finding ways to demonstrate those skills to the world in a compelling way.

People think a degree will do this for them, but it won't. Even those who have a college degree need something better. If a degree is the most interesting thing about someone, they're in trouble!

Help your child get creative and build a body of work that demonstrates who they are and what they can do. The more exposure to the real world of work they can have—and the earlier they can have it—the better. It may turn out that college or other more traditional approaches are necessary for what they want to do, but don't just assume that off the bat. You'd be surprised how much more and better your child can do than the standard approach.

What was once considered the safe route—a traditional degree followed by a stable corporate job—is no longer the sure bet it once was perceived to be (nor is all that attractive to many of the next generation). The ability to create value, solve problems, and adapt to change are becoming the new pathways to success. The entrepreneurial path, which we regularly call the ultimate education experience, is not only challenging and exciting, but it is also increasingly necessary. We are witnessing a profound shift in the landscape of risk and reward. In a world where industries can be disrupted overnight, blindly following the traditional route is now becoming the riskier choice. The greatest risk is to not take any risks at all. Cultivating an open, entrepreneurial mindset—one that embraces challenges and seeks out opportunities—is crucial. Whether your child becomes a startup founder, a skilled tradesperson, or pursues a more traditional career, these skills will be invaluable no matter what path they take.

As parents and educators, our role is to encourage this mindset, provide opportunities for real-world learning, and support children as they navigate

> *In a world where industries can be disrupted overnight, blindly following the traditional route is now becoming the riskier choice. The greatest risk is to not take any risks at all.*

their unique paths. By embracing the open education mindset, we are empowering all young people to shape their own future.

CHAPTER 10 RECAP:

- Entrepreneurial projects help students develop continuous curiosity, problem-solving skills, resilience, and interdisciplinary thinking.
- An IBM executive once said that he would rather hire a failed entrepreneur than an MBA.
- Start with the why and align your learning journey with your core values and aspirations.
- Southern New Hampshire University (SNHU-CBE) partners with OpenEd to provide access to high school students to earn a college degree.
- We are big believers in doing what we call "working out loud"—sharing their learning process and insights as they go.

BEYOND THE BOX:
THE GREAT EDUCATION UNBUNDLING

In 2022, Arizona officially became the first state to offer universal Education Savings Accounts (ESAs) to all families, regardless of income or circumstance. These state-funded accounts, called Empowerment Scholarship Accounts in Arizona, give parents flexible spending power over their children's education dollars. But this newfound freedom wasn't without its critics. In November 2023, a simple tweet about LEGO bricks ignited an unexpected firestorm in Arizona's education debate.

"I'm furious hearing that vouchers can be used to buy $500 LEGO sets for a home," wrote Jimmy, a middle school math teacher who had spent a month applying for a grant to buy off-brand LEGO-like bricks for math manipulatives that he wanted to use with the hundreds of students he taught each year.

The Cost of Education

We understand this teacher's frustration. Why should any educator have to write grants and beg for basic learning tools? Why do we trust parents who get ESAs to make educational choices but not trust teachers in traditional classrooms?

Derrell Bradford, an educational choice reformer and founder of 50CAN, saw the situation differently. "If you want to make it easier for public school teachers to purchase things like ESA families do, then ESAs are not the problem. Public school spending rules for teachers are the issue. Start there," Bradford responded.[49] The real problem, he pointed out, wasn't that families had too much freedom, it was that teachers had too little.

This debate over plastic bricks might seem trivial, but it reveals something profound about how we think about education, learning, and trust. Who gets to decide what counts as educational? Why do we trust some people to make choices but not others? And when does a toy become a learning tool?

Isaac has a rather personal interest in this debate. Between the ages of about four and thirteen, he spent roughly half of his time playing with LEGO. He was homeschooled, and though his mom really wanted to have a highly structured and rigorous curriculum for her children, she was raising three stubborn kids while also caring for a disabled husband. The result was that Isaac and his siblings didn't do much consistent, structured learning. His mom would sometimes assign them math work through a textbook, which they would complete and grade on their own. Isaac remembers sitting at his desk and moving through *Saxon Algebra 1/2* as fast as he could, not caring or comprehending it. He would grade it with the answer guide and fix errors, but mostly he was staring out the window at the excessively fat squirrels of the neighborhood, who he imagined were running some kind of animal cartel. The fattest of them was an albino squirrel who seemed to rule the others. He called him The Godsquirrel.

That was pretty much how it would go. Isaac would get the math out of the way (or not) and get back to his LEGO sets. His mom used to feel guilty about this. Frankly, so did Isaac. He was always a little worried that real school kids would be far ahead of him in their knowledge and skill and it might embarrass him some day. But that day never came. Real school kids suffered all day while he played with LEGO bricks, and by the time he did go to school, he realized they were no better for it. Only later did he come to realize how much more valuable playing with LEGO sets was than the little math he did, or really most of the formal instruction he had. While algebra taught him to solve for X on paper, building with LEGO bricks taught him to solve for building an X-wing without all the right pieces. While textbooks gave him gold stars for right answers, LEGO sets taught him to create actual value that others could appreciate. While formal education focused on following instructions, LEGO construction taught him to work within natural constraints while exercising creative freedom.

Escape the False Binary of Education Choice

For decades, families have been trapped in a false binary when it comes to education. You either send your kid to the local public school or, if you can afford it and like it, the local private school. Maybe you homeschool, but that means taking on everything yourself. This provides some choice, but each approach has mostly been stuck in its own box. These all-or-nothing propositions force families to pick between pre-packaged systems rather than crafting what actually works for their kids.

Part of the reason we accepted such limited choices was inertia. When we talk to parents about education options, they often stare at us as if we've suggested they build a rocket in their backyard. "You can do that?" they ask, bewildered by the idea that they could combine different educational approaches. This freedom of choice could be likened to the first time someone said you could order off-menu at a restaurant. You always thought you had to pick exactly what was listed, never realizing you could ask the chef to modify dishes or combine elements. Parents do the same thing with education. They look at the standard menu of public school, private school, or homeschool, and assume those are the only options.

When COVID-19 hit, it was like suddenly the restaurant kitchen was exposed. Parents saw behind the curtain of their kids' education for the first time. They watched their 2nd grader breeze through math in 20 minutes but struggle for hours with writing. They noticed their teenager come alive during hands-on projects but zone out during lectures. They realized their kindergartener learned better after running around outside, rather than after sitting still for hours. The stark reality of virtual learning laid bare the limitations of closed education. Parents paying substantial private school tuition found themselves questioning the value proposition. Why spend $12,000 or more annually just to have their child sitting at home on a laptop? Many began exploring more intimate, personalized alternatives like microschools, where smaller groups could maintain both safety and engagement. Families that never would have considered alternative education approaches started asking, "Why not?"

> *It turns out that when you start becoming an education designer, you begin seeing learning opportunities everywhere.*

A mother in Utah combined morning homeschool with afternoon enrichment classes at the local school district. A father in Florida enrolled his son in a microschool two days a week and supplemented it with online courses and sports leagues. It turns out that when you start becoming an education designer, you begin seeing learning opportunities everywhere. The à la carte revolution emerged organically from millions of families who, faced with closed schools and remote learning, began crafting solutions that actually worked for their kids. They became education designers by necessity, and many discovered they were pretty good at it.

❖ ———————————— ❖

To understand why Jimmy's LEGO tweet sparked such lively debate, and why the word "vouchers" remains such a lightning rod in the world of education reform, let's return to the free-market economist Milton Friedman who pioneered the idea that parents should be able to take the money the state would spend on their child's education and use it at the school of their choice. If you want to improve education, Friedman proffered, put purchasing power in the hands of families. Competition and choice increase quality and drive down prices in virtually every other marketplace. Why should education be different? But Friedman's design was missing a few fundamental pieces.

Imagine you could only buy groceries from one of two stores in town: the public supermarket assigned by your zip code, or the private market across town that costs twice as much. That's essentially what traditional school choice with a single-source voucher looked like. You could pick between your zoned public school or perhaps a single private school option (if the voucher covered the steep tuition difference). But for many families, these two options wouldn't have significantly expanded choice. Critics pointed to a cream-skimming effect, where only the most resourceful parents could navigate the dual choice system, leaving other families with fewer options and potentially weakening public schools in the process.

In 1970, a radical thinker named Ivan Illich held up one of the missing pieces in his book *Deschooling Society*. What if, instead of just choosing between institutions, learners could connect directly with teachers, resources, and each other through what he called "learning webs"? He imagined four networks:

1. A catalog of learning materials anyone could access
2. Skill exchanges where people could teach what they know
3. Peer-matching to find others wanting to learn the same things
4. A directory of teachers rated by previous learners

It sounded utopian at the time. The institutions were too entrenched. The idea of learning without schools seemed dangerous, maybe even anarchic. While the technology of Illich's era—limited to landline phones and printed directories—couldn't fully realize his vision, he was remarkably prescient. He anticipated the transformative power of digital networks decades before the internet, describing interconnected learning webs that mirror today's online educational platforms and social learning communities.

Today, we live in Illich's world, we just don't realize it. Want to learn guitar? YouTube has thousands of teachers. Interested in physics? Coursera and Khan Academy have you covered. Looking for a tutor? Outschool connects you with teachers reviewed by hundreds of families. The digital revolution has transformed how we access knowledge and connect with learning resources. This is how Education Savings Accounts have evolved from the old-school vouchers of Friedman's era. Instead of just picking between School A and School B, parents get digital wallets they can use for any educational expense such as personal tutoring, learning pods, specialized therapy, curriculum materials, online courses, even (gasp!) LEGO sets.

＊━━━━━━━━＊

The impact of this evolution is already visible in enrollment numbers. According to the Brookings Institution, public schools have lost over 1.2 million students since 2020. You might think this was just parents fleeing COVID policies, but look closer. Even after the pandemic, many of those families never came back. Meanwhile, many other states have passed programs like Arizona's universal ESA, giving parents flexible funding for their children's education.

According to a Forbes article by Patrick Gleason from January, 2025:

> At the beginning of 2020, there were education savings account (ESA) programs operating in only five states, while approximately a dozen states offered parents access to private school vouchers...There are now 17 states offering

ESAs and 16 states with private school voucher programs. Eligibility for those school choice programs is universal in a dozen states.[50]

In just half a decade, education savings accounts have transformed from being viewed as a fringe idea to becoming mainstream policy across America. The pace of this transformation would have seemed impossible just a few years ago.

Public schools aren't taking this lying down, nor should they. They have every natural advantage including vast campuses and buildings, stable funding, trained staff, beloved sports teams, and strong incumbency bias on the part of parents who rely on them for equal parts education and childcare. They're like the established restaurant in town that's been serving the same menu for decades. Everyone knows it, most people like it fine, and it's convenient. But as any business learning to compete in a changing market knows, advantages mean nothing if you stop meeting the needs of your customers. Think about Blockbuster facing Netflix, or taxi companies confronting Uber. Having buildings and infrastructure doesn't matter if people want something different.

The smartest districts are adapting, and it's fascinating to watch. In Tennessee, the Samuel Everett School of Innovation (a public school) pioneered a hybrid model where students attend in-person one day a week and learn from home the other four. Teachers introduce material in focused, efficient classroom sessions, and families support the learning at home. The results?

Over 90% of teachers report being satisfied with their jobs, compared to just 18% of teachers nationally. Other public systems are experimenting too. Gwinnett County, Georgia offers hybrid learning for advanced high school classes, letting students combine rigorous academics with flexible schedules. Dallas Hybrid Prep in Texas became the state's first public hybrid school by design, serving grades 3-8. Some districts are going even further, reimagining what public education can be. Several of Utah's districts are leading this transformation by participating directly in the state's ESA marketplace. They offer à la carte enrollment through the Utah Fits All Scholarship program, letting families use their education dollars to build custom combinations of public school offerings. Want to take just orchestra and physics? You can do that. Want to combine public school sports with home-based learning? No problem. These innovative districts have realized they can be part of the solution rather than resisting the change.

> *These innovative districts have realized they can be part of the solution rather than resisting the change.*

But perhaps the most fascinating story is unfolding in Utah more broadly. When the state launched its ESA program, something unexpected happened. In most states with these programs, the vast majority of families just use the funds for private school tuition, essentially treating them like traditional vouchers. Utah, however, is different. Thanks in large part to OpenEd's 16-year presence in the state, families who received the Utah Fits All ESA scholarship were already comfortable with mixing and matching educational ingredients. Many had already been experimenting with customized education. Through word of mouth at soccer fields and grocery stores, parents shared stories about crafting personalized learning approaches.

"Did you know you can combine these online classes with that science program?"

"Have you tried the coding club at the library?"

They had been practicing the art of education design long before those specific ESA funds were available. The result was that when Utah's program launched, nearly 80% of families receiving scholarships customized their children's education rather than simply paying tuition to a single private school provider.[51] Given the choice between sending their kids to a $12,000-a-year private school or crafting their own combination of learning experiences, many families chose the latter. They had learned that they could often create a better educational experience for their kids at a fraction of what private schools were spending per pupil.

As education innovator, Michael Horn points out that this mirrors what happens in every market as it matures. "Think about the Henry Ford Model T," he explained on *The OpenEd Podcast*. "At first, people said, 'Any color as long as it's black. That's great, it's an automobile.' But as soon as people started to realize they could choose different colors or seating arrangements, customization became the norm. Suddenly, choice becomes more viable as consumers get more experience with it," Horn observes.

Families across the country aren't just choosing different schools, they're becoming education designers. They are learning to combine ingredients in ways that work better for their kids, often at a fraction of what private schools charge. It's like the difference between ordering take-out every night and learning to cook. Sure, restaurants are convenient, but once you know your way around the kitchen, you can create exactly what your family loves.

> *Families aren't just choosing; they're becoming education designers.*

But there's a catch . . . and it's a big one. While parents are increasingly ready to customize, the marketplaces aren't quite there yet. Most state ESA programs are centrally administered, with all the efficiency of the local DMV. They operate like a clunky government website from 2002. Imagine if Amazon's marketplace was just a PDF list of sellers with phone numbers. That's basically what we have now. Perhaps this is why most parents still default to private school tuition, simply because it's easier than navigating bureaucratic mazes to craft custom solutions.

As Michael Horn points out, this is more than just inefficient bureaucracy, it's a fundamental market design problem. "I've seen a lot of microschools and other options that don't feel like they have sustainable business models past year two or three," he explains. "It's often teachers saying, 'I'll volunteer my time for a year.' But that's not what we want. We want you to make a living doing this, to have it work out for mutual benefit for everyone."

At OpenEd, we imagine a world where your child's education looks less like a factory assembly line and more like a bustling marketplace. Picture retired engineers teaching robotics from their garages. Local artists running weekend workshops. That teenager who is scary-good at calculus helping other kids crack the code. The mechanic who loves explaining how engines work. The librarian who starts a creative writing circle. This is what education could look like—should look like—if we built true marketplaces instead of bureaucratic processing centers.

> *At OpenEd, we imagine a world where your child's education looks less like a factory assembly line and more like a bustling marketplace.*

However, some question whether all these choices are really necessary. There is a valid critique of all forms of school choice, voiced by many open educators. The concern is that any form of government money will come with heavy strings attached and thereby limit educational freedom. Critics often say, "It's better to avoid these types of programs altogether." This is an important, consistent, and respectable position. Those who don't want anything to do with government schools, funds, or programs ought to be (and largely are in most states) free to stay away from them. We have the utmost respect for those with moral or practical reasons for avoiding any and all government education programs or resources. Keep opening your kids' education your way.

The freedom these families enjoy can produce some profound effects not seen in the same degree in even the best government-sponsored programs:

- **Extreme resourcefulness of parents**: When all you have is a few hundred dollars per kid to work with, you find ways to make it work. Homeschool moms are one of the most resourceful groups on the planet.

- **Strong voluntary community ties:** When you have to band together, and every problem requires you to leave it unsolved or solve it yourself, you get strong networks of committed families.
- **Lower priced educational options:** Without "free" money from the state, service providers competing for homeschool customers have to be as lean as possible.
- **A full flowering of experimentation:** With no state restrictions or mandates, a broader range of educational approaches evolves.

Others feel that, since they are being taxed for government schools already, getting some of those funds back in the form of vouchers, tax credits, or ESAs is a practical way to not be forced to pay double for your child's education. They feel that, since it's unlikely the government will completely get out of the business of education, it's better that education offers *more* openness, freedom, competition, and choice than less.

Still others believe strongly that the government ought to provide educational options to as many as possible, that public education is vital to ensure access for all kids, and that a more open approach accomplishes this best. This book is not about the pros and cons of any of these beliefs or approaches. In fact, even Matt and Isaac have different takes on this. Whatever your belief on the role of government in education, two things are abundantly clear: 1) students should come first and 2) parents should be the primary drivers of their kids' education.

Trust in the Learning Marketplace

Skeptics raise valid concerns about the vision of an expanded education landscape. Many wonder how such a marketplace can ensure that education providers are legitimate and that they actually provide quality outcomes for kids. These are fair concerns. Nobody wants to hand over education dollars to a fraudster.

In other areas of life, such as childcare, health care, home care, and senior care, there are systems for vetting providers. Even the vendors who sell food at farmer's markets undergo an approval process. Just like how review sites like Yelp and Google Reviews help consumers make informed decisions about restaurants and services, reputation-based systems could help parents evaluate education providers. Similar frameworks for education providers can be built while maintaining the organic, human-scale interactions that make learning come alive. If platforms like Airbnb can provide the tools and insights to book a safe lodging experience, surely there could be a similar platform created to help parents find exactly the tools, services, and curricula their child needs. To make that happen, the marketplace needs to empower passionate experts to become educational entrepreneurs.

> *Open education represents the ultimate classroom; where learning can happen anywhere, and school becomes just one of many places where knowledge comes to life.*

Open education represents the ultimate classroom; where learning can happen anywhere, and school becomes just one of many places where knowledge comes to life. There is a deeply ingrained belief that real learning only happens in structured, controlled environments with clear instructions and predetermined outcomes. But we have seen and experienced firsthand how kids thrive when adults trust them with creative freedom within safe boundaries. Just like those LEGO bricks—standardized pieces that enable infinite possibilities—the pieces themselves are rigorously quality controlled and the connections are precisely engineered. What you build with them is up to you.

The education system needs an open view of how learning happens and a creative approach to helping kids thrive in the ways that work best for them. It's not a free-for-all where anything goes; but a well-designed system of quality-tested pieces that can be combined in countless ways. We all want high standards, not suffocating standardization.

What's ironic about the middle school math teacher's complaint (that we used to open the chapter) is that he wasn't outraged about the lack of educational value of LEGO bricks. No, he saw the value of manipulative building blocks beyond mere plastic brick toys. Jimmy's frustration revealed something deeper than just a debate about LEGO bricks. It was about trust, or rather, the lack of it. He struggled to trust parents to make good educational choices, just as his administrators didn't trust him with basic purchasing decisions. Isn't this the same lack of trust that keeps many parents from letting their kids take the lead in their own education? The system has created a circular chain of distrust where bureaucrats don't trust teachers, teachers don't trust parents, and parents don't trust bureaucrats. Sadly, the natural curiosity and creativity that kids yearn to express is the price we all pay.

The reality is that kids thrive when parents and teachers trust them with creative freedom within appropriate boundaries. In the next chapter, we will explore how to start building your own educational approach. Whether you have access to ESA funds or not, whether you're working within a traditional school system or completely outside it, you can begin opening up your child's education. Like those LEGO master builders, it starts with understanding the basic pieces and learning how they fit together.

CHAPTER 11 RECAP:

- For decades, families have been trapped in a false binary when it comes to education: public or private school.
- There are now 17 states offering ESAs to families. Parents across the country aren't just choosing different schools, they're becoming education designers.

- Public schools aren't taking this lying down, nor should they. Innovative districts have realized they can be part of the solution rather than resisting the change.

- At OpenEd, we imagine a world where your child's education looks like a bustling marketplace.

- Open education represents the ultimate classroom; where learning can happen anywhere, and school becomes just one of many places where knowledge comes to life.

CHAPTER 12:

BUILDING YOUR OPEN EDUCATION PLAN

In a previous chapter, we explored how wildly popular toy bricks became an unlikely lightning rod in the education funding debate. There is one last LEGO lesson we would like to share with families considering an open education approach with their children. It's the journey from instruction-follower to Master Builder.

Lessons Learned from The LEGO Movie

If you haven't seen *The LEGO Movie* (we really hope you do!), the film centers around a construction worker named Emmet. When we first meet Emmet, he lives his life entirely by the instruction manual. "Instructions come first," he cheerfully declares, following every rule to the letter. He is so committed to doing things the right way that when faced with a crisis, he freezes, paralyzed by the absence of step-by-step directions. This may sound familiar to anyone who has ever visited a homeschooling expo, where you are surrounded by curriculum catalogs, scope-and-sequence charts, daily lesson planners, and educational consultants all promising the perfect roadmap to success. It's easy to get stuck in Emmet mode, searching for the official instructions that can tell you exactly how to build the perfect education.

> *It's easy to get stuck in Emmet mode, searching for the official instructions that can tell you exactly how to build the perfect education.*

In the movie, we learn that coveted "Master Builders" in the plastic universe don't see individual bricks, they see possibilities. Where Emmet sees a strict set of steps to follow, they see infinite combinations waiting to be discovered. "The only rule is to be awesome!" as the movie puts it. (There is actually a surprisingly profound moment where Emmet learns that the instructions he's been following aren't the source of creativity, they're often what blocks it.)

That's what fascinated us most about the LEGO debate we discussed earlier. It wasn't really about plastic bricks at all, it was about the difference between seeing education as a product on a shelf—neatly packaged with promises of guaranteed results—and seeing it as that familiar bin of mixed-up LEGO pieces in most family rooms, full of infinite creative potential. What struck us was how many families in Utah—where customized education has grown rapidly over the last 16 years—when given the freedom to choose, didn't just buy the box, they combined pieces from different sets to build something entirely new.

"Okay, but how do I actually do this?" parents often ask. "How do I design an open education plan that combines structure and creativity? Where are the instructions for building without instructions?"

That is exactly what this chapter is about. We're going to put together everything we've learned to think like Master Builders of open education. We will review the basic bricks, discover how to combine them in creative ways, and learn that following some instructions isn't such a bad thing. The goal isn't to throw away the instructions altogether, it's to reach the point where you can look at them as guidelines, not commandments, follow them when useful, and remix them when needed. So, turn on your imagination and let's start building!

Building Your Own Open Education Plan

Remember that feeling when you first dump out a huge bin of LEGO bricks? That electric mix of possibility and mild panic? That's exactly how most parents feel when first considering open education. There are so many pieces, so many possibilities. Where do you even start?

Becoming an education designer starts by creating a personalized, open education plan. It's one way of making sense of all those pieces and possibilities without limiting your child's creative potential. Rather than a rigid schedule or a predetermined path, it's more like a well-organized LEGO table where you can both find and set pieces into place as you try out new things. We know what you're likely thinking, "Isn't planning the opposite of being open?" Actually, no. Planning is essential to designing a successful open education journey. By watching tens of thousands of families plan, design, and navigate their own unique paths, we've discovered that structure doesn't limit freedom, it enables it.

When you're cooking, having an organized kitchen empowers you to be more creative. You can find the ingredients you need quickly, experiment confidently, and clean up easily. An open education plan works the same way. It's not about constraining possibilities, it's about making them accessible. Just as your child grows and changes, their educational needs will evolve too. We have seen students start with complete unschooling in their early years, transition to structured homeschooling in middle childhood, then blend part-time traditional school with outside activities in their teens. Others might thrive in a microschool one year and prefer independent study the next. The beauty of a well-designed open education plan is that it can flex and transform along with your child. You're not locked into one approach for their entire educational journey.

> *The beauty of a well-designed open education plan is that it can flex and transform along with your child.*

Most teachers are so conditioned to think of education as a sequence of subjects and grade levels that they forget the most important piece—the unique child right in front of them. Traditional education is like buying a pre-made LEGO set and insisting that every child build exactly the same thing. Adopting an open education mindset when developing your plan is like starting with your child's ideas first before helping them gather the right LEGO bricks needed to create the building of their dreams.

Let's start with the basics. A well-rounded education will cover at least the three core subjects: reading, writing, and basic math. That's about as traditional as you can get. Now, before you picture dreary workbooks and endless drills, remember our Master Builder mindset. These basics are the tools, not the torture.

Reading for some might look like a child following advanced game instructions or digesting in-depth sports articles. Writing could mean creating original scripts for YouTube videos. Math might happen through coding (for older kids) or running a lemonade stand (for younger ones). One student learned to write well by transcribing the TV broadcaster's animated voice when he described a favorite football team's highlight. Another student mastered writing by documenting their board game strategies over the period of many months.

Start this journey by telling your child that learning these basics will make their life easier. No teenager wants to struggle calculating tips as a server because they skipped basic math. No adult wants to feel anxiety about sending a simple email. Almost everything else can flow naturally from your child's curiosity and interests, so avoid forcing traditional methods and instead find ways to engage with these foundational skills that actually matter to your child.

The power of an open education plan is that it doesn't treat these basics as separate from your child's interests, it weaves them together naturally from the places where fundamental skills intersect with fascination. Perhaps this is best illustrated by an analogy. Most of us would enjoy eating bread unless we were forced to eat each ingredient separately every hour.

Would you ever eat bread again if this was your daily schedule?

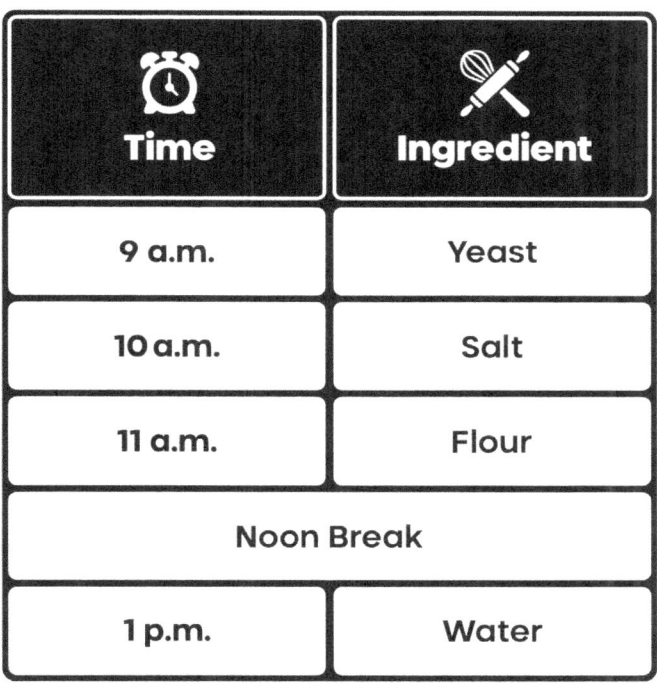

Time	Ingredient
9 a.m.	Yeast
10 a.m.	Salt
11 a.m.	Flour
Noon Break	
1 p.m.	Water

Just as you wouldn't want to consume bread ingredients separately on a rigid schedule, learning shouldn't be artificially divided into disconnected periods and subjects. Real learning, like good bread, comes from combining ingredients in meaningful ways. An open education mindset flips traditional scheduling on its head. Instead of starting with rigid periods and days of the week and trying to cram subjects into them (with children's interests squeezed into whatever time remains), an open education plan begins with the most important question of "What does your child want and need to learn?" Once you identify what you and they want and need to learn, you can then determine how they learn best, and only then do you shape the schedule to support these goals. It's a complete reversal of the traditional approach.

At the start of an open education journey, almost every family falls into the trap of trying to recreate traditional school at home; with fixed schedules all day, worksheets, textbooks, and memorization. School is familiar, and there's something oddly comforting about those neat little time blocks and orderly routines.

Take Jamie, a former classroom teacher who started her open education journey by recreating mini-school at home, complete with desks, strict schedules, and regular meltdowns. Then, one day, she found all three of her kids sprawled across a closet loft, deeply engaged in their work. The natural teacher inside her immediately thought, *"This isn't right. They need proper desks."* Then, she had the epiphany of *"Why do they have to learn at a desk at all?"* As it turned out, her daughter did her best math work at 10:30 p.m. Her son processed information better while moving. The closet loft became their favorite reading nook.

One helpful benefit of adopting an open education mindset is that you can begin working *with* your child's natural rhythms instead of *against* them. Maybe that means a sacred hour of focused learning when your child is naturally most alert; breaking up lessons into shorter chunks throughout the day; or letting your night owl tackle complex problems after dark. The goal isn't to abolish all structure, it's to create the right structure for your unique child. One that respects their natural learning patterns instead of forcing them into an arbitrary mold.

Let's look at how different families have discovered their rhythm and created schedules that blend a variety of ingredients into something meaningful. Here are some fictional archetypes based on the 100,000+ students who have passed through the OpenEd program.

Sample Plans Based on Real Families

Jake, the Maker (Age 8)

Jake is a natural builder and inventor who lights up when he's creating things. While he struggled with sitting still and following standard lessons in a traditional classroom, his parents noticed he could focus intensely for hours on building projects. He's fascinated by how things work and learns best through hands-on experimentation. Though gifted in spatial reasoning and engineering thinking, he sometimes avoids reading and writing tasks.

WHAT Jake wants to learn this year:

- Building and engineering fundamentals to support his maker interests
- Key math concepts, especially geometry and measurement
- Reading and writing (integrated naturally through his projects)
- Basic digital design skills
- Science concepts through hands-on experiments

HOW he'll learn it:

- Synthesis Tutor, a game-based math program developed in-house at SpaceX's experimental school
- Local makerspace membership for hands-on learning and community
- Teaching Textbooks for math, chosen for its visual, interactive approach
- Project documentation to develop writing skills naturally
- Digital design software basics for planning builds
- Science experiments tied to building interests

- Movement-friendly approaches (building breaks, hands-on materials)
- Regular maker showcases to share projects

WHEN it works best (some activities have fixed times):

- Tuesday/Thursday, 10:00 a.m.: Makerspace workshops with other young inventors
- Wednesday, 2:00 p.m.: Science club at the local library
- Friday, 3:00 p.m.: Digital design mentor session

The rest flows naturally around these anchors:

- Morning quiet time for math and reading
- Project work between scheduled activities
- Movement/outdoor play breaks as needed throughout the day

This plan adapts to Jake's energy levels and interests while ensuring he develops essential skills through activities that engage him. Rather than forcing traditional methods that previously caused frustration, this approach harnesses his natural maker mindset to fuel learning across all areas.

Emma, the Dancer (Age 14)

Emma has been training in classical ballet since age four and shows exceptional promise. Now, preparing for international competitions and summer intensives, she needs an education plan that supports her rigorous dance training while maintaining strong academics.

WHAT Emma wants to learn this year:

- Full college-prep academic curriculum
- Advanced ballet technique and repertoire

- Dance history and theory
- French language (important for ballet terminology)
- Anatomy and nutrition

HOW she'll learn it:

- Subject curriculum for core academics (enables flexible yet comprehensive study)
- Professional ballet training at City Ballet Academy
- Private French tutoring
- Online anatomy courses focused on dance
- Performance preparation and rehearsals

WHEN it happens (Ballet Academy schedule - fixed):

- Monday to Friday, 7:30 to 9:30 a.m.: Morning technique class
- Monday, Wednesday, and Friday, 2:00 to 4:30 p.m.: Repertoire and variations
- Tuesday and Thursday, 2:00 to 4:00 p.m.: Pointe and partnering
- Saturday, 9:00 a.m. to 1:00 p.m.: Rehearsals for upcoming performances

Academic Schedule (works around ballet):

- Subject curriculum coursework: 10:00 a.m. to 1:30 p.m.
- Evenings: Homework and additional studying
- Sunday: Rest day and catch-up on academics as needed
- French tutor: Tuesday and Thursday, 4:30 p.m.
- Anatomy course: Self-paced during academic block

Emma's schedule is necessarily more structured due to her professional training requirements, but still maintains flexibility for academic work within her demanding dance schedule.

Marika, the Citizen Scientist (Age 10)

Marika has always been happiest outdoors. Her parents noticed early on that her curiosity and focus skyrocketed during nature activities when she could spend hours observing birds or collecting plant samples. While initially quiet in group settings, she has become increasingly confident, leading nature walks and sharing her knowledge with others. She is particularly passionate about water conservation and local wildlife.

WHAT Marika wants to learn this year:

- Environmental science with focus on local ecosystems
- Data collection and analysis skills
- Writing and communication (through nature journalism)
- Essential math concepts through real-world application
- Basic coding for citizen science projects
- Leadership skills through community involvement

HOW she'll learn it:

- Weekly field studies with local naturalist group
- Water quality monitoring project with county scientists
- Nature journaling curriculum for writing development
- Math-U-See program integrated with field data collection
- Citizen science apps and online data submission
- Leadership role in Junior Rangers program
- Monthly nature photography workshops

WHEN it happens (some activities have fixed times):

- Monday, 9:00 a.m.: Volunteer at wildlife rehabilitation center
- Tuesday and Thursday, 10:00 a.m.: Nature study group
- Wednesday, 1:00 p.m.: Water quality monitoring team

- First Saturday: Junior Rangers leadership program
- Last Friday: Photography workshop with local nature photographer

Flexible flow:

- Early mornings: Bird watching and nature journaling
- Core academics between field activities
- Seasonal adjustments for migration patterns and weather
- Monthly showcase of findings to community environmental group

Marika's plan demonstrates how a passion for nature can drive learning across multiple subjects while contributing to real scientific research and community conservation efforts. Her schedule adapts to both structured commitments and natural phenomena like migrations and seasonal changes.

Zain, the Game Designer (Age 12)

Zain can explain in intricate detail how he redesigned a popular video game to be more accessible for his cousin who has limited mobility. That's Zain in a nutshell—a kid who sees technology not just as entertainment, but as a way to solve real problems. Though his previous school labeled him as distracted, it turns out he was just itching to create, rather than consume.

WHAT Zain wants to learn this year:

- Game design and basic programming
- Storytelling and narrative design
- Project management skills
- Advanced math concepts (especially for game mechanics)
- Inclusive design principles
- Marketing and community building

HOW he'll learn it:

- Online game development course with mentor
- Creative writing workshop focused on interactive stories
- Math curriculum focused on game mechanics and statistics
- Weekly play-testing sessions with diverse user group
- Regular meetings with accessibility experts
- Building a portfolio of small games

WHEN it happens (fixed points):

- Tuesday and Thursday, 10:00 a.m.: Online coding classes
- Wednesday, 2:00 p.m.: Creative writing workshop
- Friday, 3:00 p.m.: Play-testing group
- Monthly accessibility consultation

Flexible flow:

- Morning focus time for academics
- Afternoon project work
- Evening gaming research (studying successful games)
- Regular breaks for physical activity

The Chen Siblings: (Lily, age 9 and James, age7)

Here is a fascinating case of two siblings who couldn't be more different, yet their parents have found a beautiful way to weave their learning together. Lily is a born performer who processes everything through movement and music, while James is a methodical tinkerer who loves taking things apart. Instead of running two separate schedules, their family created a harmonious plan that plays to both their strengths.

WHAT each of them want to learn this year:

Lily:

- Musical theater and dance
- Story creation through movement
- Math through music theory
- Physical science through dance

James:

- Engineering and mechanics
- Math through building
- Communication through project documentation
- Sound and physics

Together:

- Collaborative projects combining performance and technical elements
- Essential reading and writing skills
- Basic Spanish

HOW they'll learn it:

- Musical theater program (Lily leads, James runs tech)
- Maker projects (James leads, Lily adds creative elements)
- Shared math curriculum with different applications
- Joint Spanish learning through songs and building projects
- Regular "show and teach" sessions where they teach each other

WHEN it happens (fixed schedule):

- Monday and Wednesday, 9:00 a.m.: Theater program
- Tuesday and Thursday, 10:00 a.m.: Maker workshop

- Friday morning: Spanish immersion playgroup
- Saturday: Family project time

Flexible elements:

- Morning academic skills work
- Afternoon individual passion projects
- Evening family sharing and planning
- Regular collaboration time for their productions

Amara, the Journalist (Age 15)

Amara told her parents she wanted to start a youth-focused news podcast. She wasn't interested in TikTok fame. Instead, she wanted to help kids understand what was happening in their world. Her passion for storytelling and truth-seeking has shaped an education plan that's rigorous yet deeply meaningful to her.

WHAT Amara wants to learn this year:

- Journalism ethics and practices
- World events and history
- Advanced writing and editing
- Audio production
- Interview techniques
- Statistics and data analysis
- Media literacy

HOW she'll learn it:

- Online journalism courses
- Mentorship with local reporter
- History through current events
- Writing workshops

- Statistics through data journalism
- Weekly podcast production
- Youth journalism network

WHEN it happens (fixed commitments):

- Monday, 9:00 a.m.: Editorial meeting with youth news network
- Tuesday and Thursday: Writing workshop
- Wednesday: Interview skills training
- Friday: Podcast recording and production

Daily rhythm:

- Early morning: News reading and research
- Mid-morning: Academic work
- Afternoon: Story development and interviews
- Evening: Audio editing and production
- Breaking news: Schedule flexes as needed

Sarah, the Renaissance Kid (Age 15)

Sarah had been homeschooling for years, but missed certain aspects of traditional school, particularly the energy of group performances and team sports. What emerged was a fascinating blend of independent learning and school involvement that perfectly captured her multi-passionate nature.

WHAT Sarah wants to learn this year:

- Advanced mathematics (she dreams of designing stage sets)
- Musical performance and composition
- Visual arts and design
- Athletic development through volleyball

- Business skills (she runs a small custom jewelry line)
- Core academics with college prep focus

HOW she'll learn it:

- Split enrollment with local high school for specific programs
- Independent study for core subjects
- Private art instruction
- Business mentorship
- Online courses for flexibility
- Community involvement

WHEN it happens: School-based commitments:

- Monday: 7:30 to 8:45 a.m.: Advanced orchestra at high school
- Thursday: 9:00 to 10:30 a.m.: AP Chemistry (the labs were too good to pass up!)
- Friday: 3:00 to 5:30 p.m.: Varsity volleyball practice

Independent learning flow:

- Late morning: Core academics and college prep
- Early afternoon: Art and design work
- Evening: Jewelry business operations
- Weekends: Community performances and volleyball tournaments

Sarah's story completely shatters the either/or mentality about education. Her family didn't have to choose between "school" and "not school." They created a third path that took the best of both worlds. Some days Sarah can be found in a chemistry lab with her school friends, other days she's deep in her home studio, working on commissioned artwork. This kind of hybrid approach often raises questions about working with school districts.

Many parents worry their district won't allow part-time enrollment or that they will face resistance. When approaching your district, if they express reservations, start by responding, "Thank you for your concern. I believe this is what's best for my child at this time. How many classes can my child take as a part-time student at this school?"

If they respond with, "None. You must choose one way or the other," don't get discouraged. Most states allow some version of part-time enrollment, especially for students in grades 7-12. Here's how to overcome this hurdle:

1. Research your state's education laws regarding "dual enrollment" between homeschooling and public schooling.
2. Document your request and responses in writing.
3. Approach multiple levels of administration if needed.
4. Stay positive and persistent.

You are not asking for special treatment, you're requesting access to public education resources that your tax dollars already support. Many districts initially resist flexible arrangements out of habit rather than policy. Polite persistence often reveals more options than first offered.

> *Polite persistence often reveals more options than first offered.*

Making it Click Together

Like any good LEGO build, your open education journey starts with a few basic pieces. Begin with something that excites your child—maybe a new math program that speaks to their interests, or a weekly nature club that gets them outdoors. Give each new piece time to settle into place. Most OpenEd families have found a month is usually enough to see if something truly clicks. As you experiment, you will start recognizing patterns. One child might

> *Like any good LEGO build, your open education journey starts with a few basic pieces. Begin with something that excites your child.*

tackle complex problems better in the morning. Another child tends to grasp mathematical concepts more easily through hands-on projects than with textbooks. For other learners, the exact opposite could be true!

Set up simple check-ins, a quick weekly chat about what's working, plus a deeper monthly review. Watch for the signals that matter such as growing curiosity, rising confidence, and genuine engagement. Remember that productive struggle often looks different from real frustration. Sometimes, what appears to be easy success might actually be a sign your child is ready for bigger challenges.

Building your support network makes everything easier. Connect with local families through homeschool groups, community centers, or social media. Many families create informal learning pods where kids can learn together, sharing resources and responsibilities. Some divide teaching duties based on their strengths, while others collectively hire tutors or specialists for specific subjects.

To help you organize all these pieces, we've curated a free set of tools and resources for you at opened.co/book. Whether you use our tool or create your own system, what matters is having a way to track your journey and plan your next steps. Think of it like sorting your LEGO collection. Good organization makes creative building possible.

We started this chapter talking about the difference between seeing LEGO as a product on a shelf versus a bin of infinite possibilities. Your child's education is the same way. You don't have to follow the picture on someone else's box or splurge to purchase all the latest fancy curricula. Chances are, you already have most of the pieces you need to build something remarkable right at your fingertips.

CHAPTER 12 RECAP:

- Becoming an education designer starts by creating a personalized, open education plan along with your support network.

- Begin working *with* your child's natural rhythms instead of *against* them.

- Like any good LEGO build, your open education journey starts with a few basic pieces. Begin with something that excites your child.

- You likely already have most of the pieces you need to build something remarkable today!

CONCLUSION:

YOU CAN DO THIS (YOU ALREADY ARE)

An Ode to Sir Ken Robinson

In 2007, the late, great Sir Ken Robinson took the stage at TED and asked a simple question, "Do schools kill creativity?"[52] The talk became a phenomenon, racking up over 100 million views in the first 15 years. But what's truly fascinating isn't the talk itself, it's the comments that have accumulated over the years.

Here is one from 2016: "Almost 10 years since this video was posted and unfortunately nothing has changed."

Fast forward two years: "Clap clap. 12 years have gone by, we're still in the same boat."

After Robinson's passing in 2020, the video received a renewed flood of attention, and the chorus of frustration remains the same: "It's incredibly upsetting how old this is and how everything is still the same."

The frustration is palpable. Year after year, decade after decade, audiences nod along to calls for educational transformation. They attend conferences, read books about reimagining learning, and share social media posts about how the system needs to change. Robinson wasn't just another talking head with opinions about education. Knighted in 2003 for his service to the arts, he had advised governments, non-profits, and Fortune 500 companies on creative and cultural education. His message struck a chord because it named something many had felt but couldn't articulate. We seem to be stuck with an industrial-age model of education in a post-industrial world.

> *"We don't grow into creativity, we get educated out of it." —Sir Ken Robinson*

"Our education system has mined our minds in the way that we strip-mine the earth for a particular commodity," Robinson observed. His most radical claim was that we don't grow into creativity, we get educated out of it.

What those YouTube commenters missed is that while they were waiting for the system to transform, tens of thousands of families quietly started building something new. They didn't wait for permission or wait for reform. They just started where they were, with what they had. A mother in Utah realized her daughter learned better through movement, so she found a dance program that integrated academic concepts. A father in Oregon noticed his son's passion for video games could teach programming skills. A group of families in Michigan created a learning pod before anyone had even coined the term. Think of the most transformative moments in your life. Chances are, they didn't happen by following a predetermined path. They came from taking a leap, from daring to do things differently. Embracing an open education mindset can feel like a big leap, one that could redefine not just your child's learning, but your entire family's approach to education. You can do it!

Throughout this book, we've explored the building blocks of open education through the lens of different approaches, various tools, and stories of families that have found their way. If you feel a bit overwhelmed right now, wondering if you can really do this, we have something important to tell you. You likely already are doing it.

Remember that time you followed your child's curiosity about space and ended up spending a whole weekend exploring astronomy? That was open education. When you let your kid redesign their bedroom and helped them calculate materials and costs? That was open education too. Every time you've supported your child's interests, adapted to their learning style, or created opportunities for real-world learning, you have practiced the principles we've discussed. We have seen time and again how this approach transforms entire family dynamics. Parents who initially felt overwhelmed by the idea of guiding their child's education soon find themselves saying, "We didn't know how this would turn out, but we've discovered we're capable of far more than we ever imagined."

Whatever your constraints, you can open up your child's education even just a little bit at a time. Whether you're in a public, private, charter, or homeschool situation, you can find ways to assess your goals, needs, resources, and options. You can expand your thinking beyond the walls of a classroom to help your child succeed. Don't ever feel that if you can't drop everything to create the perfect educational experience you're failing. Remember that the perfect education plan doesn't exist. The pursuit of authentic learning is a lifelong journey and it tends to get a bit messy along the way. Embrace it!

Take any steps you can today toward a more open education. When tasks feel overwhelming—as they often do when you're reimagining your child's entire educational approach—break them down into smaller, manageable goals. Every great movement starts small. You don't need to overhaul your entire life overnight. Start with one small change, one new approach to learning. As you gain confidence and see the positive impact on your child, you will naturally want to do more. Celebrating small wins along the way is crucial. When you can see your progress, your confidence grows.

Avoid the temptation to compare your family to others, especially social media influencers who seem to have it all under control. Remember that most of what you see on social media is staged for entertainment purposes (i.e., views, likes, and shares) and only ever shows partial reality. That perfectly curated homeschool room? It probably looked like a tornado hit it 10 minutes after the photo. Those carefully edited day-in-the-life videos? They don't show the struggles, the doubts, or the messy reality of learning. This culture of comparison feeds right into what Robinson warned us about, the fear of being wrong, the paralyzing need to do everything perfectly. Just as you shouldn't expect your children to get everything right the first time, you need to give yourself permission to experiment, to make mistakes, and to learn as you go.

We find many families who have adopted the OpenEd mindset don't realize how amazing they are precisely because they're too busy comparing themselves to an impossible standard. When we ask the Kamara family to share about the cool things they do for their children, they invariably reply, "Well, we don't really know what we're doing, but you should talk to the Johnson family as they are doing awesome stuff with their children." And guess what? Once we chat with the Johnson family, they end up saying the very same thing about the Kamaras.

When we began this book, we promised you would have the tools and confidence to create an education that nurtures your child's unique gifts. By now, you've seen how a truly open approach to education goes far beyond traditional definitions of success or failure. You understand that real learning isn't about checking boxes or following prescribed paths; it's about recognizing and nurturing the spark in each child.

> *Real learning isn't about checking boxes or following prescribed paths; it's about recognizing and nurturing the spark in each child.*

In an era where artificial intelligence and automation are transforming every industry, the skills that matter most aren't the ones that can be standardized and tested. Instead, the ability to think creatively, adapt quickly, and learn continuously are what matter most. You now have the basic framework for fostering these capabilities in your child:

- You can spot learning opportunities in everyday moments.
- You know how to build a flexible schedule that adapts to your child's needs.
- You understand how to evaluate and choose from the growing marketplace of educational options.
- You have strategies for integrating core skills into your child's natural interests.
- Most importantly, you know you are not alone on this journey.

The gap between what traditional schools teach and what the real world demands is widening. You don't have to be paralyzed by this reality. You have seen how other families are bridging this gap, creating hybrid approaches that combine the best of different worlds. You have concrete examples of how to supplement any educational setting, whether your child is in public school, private school, homeschool, or somewhere in between. The tools we have explored are already being used successfully by tens of thousands of families who, just like you, started with a mixture of hope and uncertainty. They discovered, as you will, that having all the answers upfront isn't the key to transforming your child's education experience. The key is having the confidence to take that first step, knowing you have the resources and support to figure out the next one.

While the educational system remains like a massive ship with an undersized rudder, the real innovation is happening at the edges. Parents frustrated with one-size-fits-all approaches aren't waiting for permission or system-wide reform. They are building microschools, forming learning pods, mixing virtual and in-person instruction, and creating hybrid schedules that combine the best of different worlds. As President Theodore Roosevelt reminded us, credit belongs to the person "who is actually in the arena, whose face is marred by dust and sweat and blood, who strives valiantly, who errs and comes up short again and again, because there is no

> *The open education revolution isn't coming. It's already here. And you're part of it.*

effort without error or shortcoming."[53] You are in that arena now. Every time you try something new with your child's education, every time you support their unique interests, every time you choose growth over conformity you are helping to build the future of learning.

The industrial model of education has shaped generations of learners, including many who succeeded within its confines. But that doesn't mean we're doomed to perpetuate it. Even those who thrived in traditional schools can recognize its limitations and participate in crafting something better. We just have to get creative.

You don't have to wait for system-wide change. The education revolution doesn't need another conference, policy paper, or viral video. It can start in your home, in your classroom, in your community today. Encourage creativity, especially when it leads to mistakes. Create space for discovery, even if it means deviating from the standard path. Trust that you know your child better than any system ever could. The world has changed dramatically since Ken Robinson first challenged us to rethink education. We don't have to wait another decade to see change. It's already happening, family by family, child by child, one brave choice at a time.

The open education revolution isn't coming. It's already here. And you're part of it.

Visit opened.co/book to join the movement and access additional resources.

MATT BOWMAN

Matt Bowman is an innovator in education and technology and is deeply dedicated to transforming the way children learn. He and his wife, Amy founded OpenEd together, which has collectively served more than 100,000 students over the years across multiple states, including many military families worldwide. The Bowmans have spent over three decades championing personalized education, combining cutting-edge technology with an entrepreneurial spirit to help students thrive in a rapidly changing world.

A former 6th grade teacher and tech executive, Matt has been at the forefront of online education since the 1990s. He holds a bachelor's degree and a master's degree in education and is an alumnus of Stanford's Executive Business Management program. Matt's insights into the future of education have led him to be a speaker and panelist at numerous educational and technology conferences around the world.

Matt and Amy live in the mountains of Utah, where they enjoy spending time with their five adult children and their spouses, plus four grandchildren (and counting).

ISAAC MOREHOUSE

Isaac Morehouse is the CEO of OpenEd, working to open up all education options to all learners. He has founded and built several companies, served as a CEO and CMO, and loves rallying people around a vision and building teams to do the things he can't.

Isaac is dedicated to the relentless pursuit of freedom and is deeply passionate about education and entrepreneurship. He loves writing, music, his wife Heather and four kids, a good cigar, and getting angry about sports (especially the Detroit Lions).

He has given hundreds of talks and interviews, authored, co-authored, or ghostwritten over 3,000 articles and twelve books, helped thousands of people launch their careers, and dozens of businesses tell their stories. He is a firm believer in learning out loud and making a daily commitment to creation in all forms.

He currently lives with his family in Bradenton, Florida.

ACKNOWLEDGMENTS

From Matt: First and foremost, I want to thank my wife, Amy, who not only co-founded OpenEd with me but has also been the heart and soul of our mission from day one. Her early contributions to this book and her constant support of our vision have been invaluable. She exemplifies the open education mindset in everything she does, starting with how she helped guide our own five children's educational journeys.

From Isaac: I am deeply grateful to my wife Heather and our children, who have been both my inspiration and my testing ground for these ideas. They have taught me more about learning and education than any research or theory ever could.

Together, we want to express our profound gratitude to the many people who helped bring this book to life. Our exceptional team of beta readers, whose insights sharpened our thinking and refined our message including Lauren Hodge, Olivia Burr, Andrea Fife, Matt Barnes, Dave Rasmussen, Avalie Muhlestein, Jon England, Katie Craig, and Valerie Harmon. Your thoughtful feedback helped ensure this book would truly serve families embarking on their open education journey.

Charlie Deist deserves special recognition for his careful editorial eye and ability to strengthen our core arguments while maintaining our authentic voices. Ela Richmond's artistic vision helped bring our concepts to life visually.

We are indebted to Anita Henderson and Jenn Foster for their expertise in guiding this book from concept to completion, helping us navigate the complex process of book production while keeping our message clear and accessible.

Most importantly, we want to thank the tens of thousands of families that have been part of the OpenEd journey. Your stories, struggles, and successes have shaped not just this book, but also our entire understanding of what education can be. To every parent who has shared their experiences on our podcast, every educator who has pushed boundaries to better serve their students, and every advocate who has helped advance the cause of educational freedom, this book exists because of you.

Finally, to all the pioneers of the open education movement—the parents, teachers, entrepreneurs, and innovators who refused to accept the status quo—your courage in charting new paths has made it easier for others to follow. This book is dedicated to you and to all the families who will join this revolution in the years to come.

END NOTES

1   Leonard Reinecke, Tilo Hartmann, and Allison Eden, "The Guilty Couch Potato: The Role of Ego Depletion in Reducing Recovery Through Media Use," *Journal of Communication* 64, no. 4 (August 2014): 569–589, https://doi.org/10.1111/jcom.12107.

2   Linda Jacobsen, "Responding to Post-Pandemic Norms, More States Are Lowering Test Standards." *The 74*, September 25, 2024. https://www.the74million.org/article/responding-to-post-pandemic-norms-more-states-are-lowering-testing-standards/.

3   Melanie Hanson, "U.S. Public Spending Statistics," Education Data Initiative, July 14, 2024, https://educationdata.org/public-education-spending-statistics

4   Penn Wharton Budget Model, "Is Income Implicit in Measures of Student Ability?" September 28, 2021, https://budgetmodel.wharton.upenn.edu/issues/2021/9/28/is-income-implicit-in-measures-of-student-ability.

5   Carl Campanile, "Almost 200k students boycotted NY state standardized tests in parents' rights revolt, New York Post, December 31, 2023, https://nypost.com/2023/12/31/metro/almost-200k-students-boycotted-ny-state-standardized-tests-in-parents-rights-revolts

6   Thomas S. Dee and Mark Murphy et al. "Patterns in the pandemic decline of public school enrollment, Educational Researcher, First published online August 11, 2021, Volume 50, Issue 8, https://doi.org/10.3102/0013189X211034481

7   Ibid

8   Michael B. Horn, "As Education Choice Grows, Expect More School Unbundling, But No Great Unbundling." Forbes, October 17, 2023. https://www.forbes.com/sites/michaelhorn/2023/10/17/as-education-choice-grows-expect-more-school-unbundling-but-no-great-unbundling/.

9   Patricia M. Lines, *Homeschoolers: Estimating Numbers and Growth* (Washington, DC: Office of Educational Research and Improvement, U.S. Department of Education, Spring 1999), 2. https://eric.ed.gov/?id=ED456167.

10   Brian D. Ray, "How Many Homeschool Students are there in the United States during the 2021-2022 School Year?" National Home Education Research Institute, September 15, 2022. https://www.nheri.org/how-many-homeschool-students-are-there-in-the-united-states.

11   Jennifer A. Heissel, Emma K. Adam et al. "Testing, Stress, and Performance: How Students Respond Psychologically to High-Stakes Testing," Education Finance & Policy, April 19, 2021   https://direct.mit.edu/edfp/article/16/2/183/97156/Testing-Stress-and-Performance-How-Students

12   Rachel Wells, "70% Of Employers Say Creative Thinking Is Most In-Demand Skill In 2024," *Forbes*, January 28, 2024, https://www.forbes.com/sites/rachelwells/2024/01/28/70-of-employers-say-creative-thinking-is-most-in-demand-skill-in-2024/

13   "Education and Socioeconomic Status," American Psychological Association, accessed October 13, 2024, https://www.apa.org/pi/ses/resources/publications/education.

14   Peter Gray, *Free to Learn: Why Unleashing the Instinct to Play Will Make Our Children Happier, More Self-Reliant, and Better Students for Life* (New York: Basic Books, 2013), 45.

15   Mimsy Sadofsky, edited version of a talk delivered at Fairfield School in Wolfeville, Nova Scotia, accessed January 15, 2025. sudburyvalley.org/essays/outcomes-0

16 Melanie Hanson, *Student Loan Debt Statistics*, Education Data Initiative, last updated March 16, 2025, https://educationdata.org/student-loan-debt-statistics.

17 Technavio, "Test Preparation Market Analysis US - Size and Forecast 2024-2028," accessed March 24, 2025, https://www.technavio.com/report/test-preparation-market-industry-in-the-us-analysis.

18 William Hermanns, *Einstein and the Poet: In Search of the Cosmic Man* (Branden Books, 2011), XX.

19 Judith Harackiewicz, Jessie L. Smith, Stacy J. Priniski, et al, "Interest Matters: The Importance of Promoting Interest in Education," *Sage Journals*, June 30, 2016, 3(2), 220–227. https://doi.org/10.1177/2372732216655542

20 Dan Ariely, *Payoff: The Hidden Logic That Shapes Our Motivations,* (TED Books, 2016), XX.

21 Chris Sturgis, "FAQ: What countries are implementing competency-based education?" *Learning Edge*, March 11, 2020, https://learningedge.me/faq-what-countries-are-implementing-competency-based-education.

22 "2024 Commencement Address by Roger Federer," Dartmouth College, accessed October 14, 2024, https://home.dartmouth.edu/news/2024/06/2024-commencement-address-roger-federer

23 Emily Stewart, "The Joy of Average," *Business Insider*, Aug. 4, 2024, https://www.businessinsider.com/consumerism-capitalism-optimization-culture-live-medium-average-good-enough-2024-8

24 Logan LaPlante, "Hackschooling makes me happy," TEDx University of Nevada, accessed October 13, 2024 https://youtu.be/h11u3vtcpaY?si=LDOhOZ9z3kgHEHUM

25 Huizhong Wu, "Chinese families seeking to escape a competitive education system have found a haven in Thailand," Associated Press, September 5, 2024, https://apnews.com/article/chinese-immigration-thailand-schools-chiang-mai-9d1953344e8b35327020408b8f677264

26 Amelia Hill, "Anne Fine: Children Should Be Allowed to Learn Online Instead of Going to School," *The Guardian*, September 7, 2024, https://www.theguardian.com/education/article/2024/sep/07/anne-fine-children-should-allowed-learn-online-instead-school.

27 "Parents Under Pressure: The U.S. Surgeon General's Advisory on the Mental Health & Well-Being of Parents," Office of the U.S. Surgeon General, 2024, https://www.hhs.gov/sites/default/files/parents-under-pressure.pdf

28 "Child Development Guide: Ages and Stages," Children's Hospital of Orange County, accessed October 15, 2024, https://choc.org/primary-care/ages-stages/.

29 "Do Twins Reach Developmental Milestones at the Same Time?" Pathways.org, accessed October 15, 2024, https://pathways.org/twin-development/

30 Lucy Bryan, Dr. Lulu Guo, "Circadian Rhythm: What it is, what it shapes, and why it's fundamental to getting quality sleep," Sleep Foundation, March 15, 2024, https://www.sleepfoundation.org/circadian-rhythm

31 Clayton M. Christensen, Taddy Hall, Karen Dillon, and David S. Duncan, *Competing Against Luck: The Story of Innovation and Customer Choice* (New York: HarperBusiness, 2016).

32 IGN, "The 10 Best-Selling Video Games of All Time," October 2023, https://www.ign.com/articles/best-selling-video-games-of-all-time-grand-theft-auto-minecraft-tetris.

33 Fatima Malik, Raman Marwaha, "Developmental Stages of Social Emotional Development in Children, National Library of Medicine, September 18, 2022, https://www.ncbi.nlm.nih.gov/books/NBK534819

34 Jonathan Haidt, (2024). *The Anxious Generation: How the Great Rewiring of Childhood Is Causing an Epidemic of Mental Illness.* Penguin Press. at, 2024)

35 Peter Gray, *Free to Learn: Why Unleashing the Instinct to Play Will Make Our Children Happier, More Self-Reliant, and Better Students for Life*, (Basic Books; 1st edition, 2013).

36 C.H. Hart, L.D. Newell, & J.H. Haupt (2008). *Love, limits, and latitude: A tailored approach to parenting. Ensign, 38*(8), 60–65.

37 "Play Digest: This Is Your Brain on Play," Peabody Essex Museum, accessed October 18, 2024, http://playtime.pem.org/play-digest-this-is-your-brain-on-play

38 J.M. Zosh, E.J. Hopkins, H. Jensen, C. Liu, D. Neale, K. Hirsh-Pasek, S.L. Solis, & D. Whitebread (2017). *Learning through play: A review of the evidence.* The LEGO Foundation. ISBN: 978-87-999589-1-7

39 "Mike Rowe Details 'Shift' in the Path to Prosperity: 'Entering a Whole New Time' of Smart Money," *Fox Business*, April 7, 2024, https://www.foxbusiness.com/lifestyle/mike-rowe-details-shift-path-prosperity-entering-whole-new-time-smart-money.

40 "Talent Disrupted: College Graduates, Underemployment, and the Way Forward," Strada Education Foundation, February 2024, https://stradaeducation.org/report/talent-disrupted/

41 Simon Sinek, *Start with Why: How Great Leaders Inspire Everyone to Take Action* (Portfolio Publishing, 2011).

42 Ibid, p. XX

43 Melanie Hanson, "Average Student Loan Debt," Education Data Initiative, August 16, 2024, https://educationdata.org/average-student-loan-debt#:~:text=The%20average%20federal%20student%20loan,have%20federal%20student%20loan%20debt.

44 "The Future of Jobs Report 2023," World Economic Forum, April 30, 2023, https://www.weforum.org/publications/the-future-of-jobs-report-2023/

45 Mike Rowe, "America is lending money it doesn't have to kids who can't pay it back to train them for jobs that no longer exist," mikeroweWORKS Foundation, accessed March 24, 2025, https://mikeroweworks.org/.

46 "U.S. Chamber Debuts Workforce Initiative," CBIA, February 18, 2022, https://www.cbia.com/news/workforce/u-s-chamber-workforce-initiative/

47 Mike Rowe, "Slightly Longer Than 5 Minute Testimony to Congress," *Mike Rowe*, March 1, 2017, https://mikerowe. com/2017/03/testimony-to-the-committee-on-education-and-the-workforce/

48 "Industry Certification: Gold Standard Career Pathways Articulation Agreements," Florida Department of Education, accessed January 28, 2025, https://www.fldoe.org/academics/career-adult-edu/career-technical-edu-agreements/industry-certification.stml

49 Derrell Bradford, (@Dyrnwyn). "I see now it's 'can be used.' If you want to make it easier for public school teachers to purchase things like ESA families do then ESAs are not the problem. Public school spending rules for teachers are the issue." Twitter, November 20, 2023. https://x.com/Dyrnwyn/status/1726781800490373626.

50 Patrick Gleason. "Large, Fast-Growing States Are Set to Expand School Choice in 2025." *Forbes*, January 14, 2025. https://www.forbes.com/sites/patrickgleason/2025/01/14/large-fast-growing-states-are-set-to-expand-school-choice-in-2025/.

51 Matt Bowman & Isaac Morehouse, hosts, "Episode 004 – The End of One-size-fits-all," OpenEd Podcast, OpenEd, February 2024, 45 min., 07 sec., https://open.spotify.com/episode/3Zm acVEOCtAPv9gS3Qb8b6?si=xUYECQ-1QHuMkHe8pAfRaw

52 "Do schools kill creativity?" Sir Ken Robinson, TED, accessed October 14, 2024, https://www.ted.com/talks/sir_ken_robinson_do_schools_kill_creativity?subtitle=en

53 Theodore Roosevelt, speech at the Paris-Sorbonne University, April 23, 1910.

www.ingramcontent.com/pod-product-compliance
Lightning Source LLC
Chambersburg PA
CBHW061145120626
46546CB00005B/1939